The questionnaire for healing triggered emotions

Stefanie Hartl

© Copyright: 2022

Stefanie Hartl

1st edition 2022

ISBN: 9798842442430

The emotional baggage is healed
and integrated into love, so that
what you are can rise in
its full bloom

Foreword

First of all, I would like to thank you for your courage to face your feelings so consciously. Not everyone finds this courage, and therefore be aware that this is a great leap of consciousness and a great path to mental healing. How wonderful that you have found it! Also, I want to mention that this book is a support and not a substitute for therapeutic treatment.

What are "triggered emotions, anyway?"

Triggers are small events, situations or words that trigger strong emotions but are way too exaggerated for that event. It's like someone is rubbing salt into your wounds without intending to. However, since these wounds are present in you, this happens again and again until you find a way to heal them. At first you believe that these people are inflicting those wounds on you and you may withdraw or seek a way with less pain (distractions, addictions, avoidance of certain situations or people, self-harm, etc). **But the right path is actually the one IN the pain.** Encountering each new pain brings you closer and closer to yourself.

For example, your boss asks you for a favor in a somewhat stern, reproachful tone and suddenly you get a violent feeling of anxiety and deep sadness. Thoughts rattle around in your head like "I will never be accepted if I don't do everything perfectly".

This fear and sadness are wounds from an earlier time in which it was essential for you to be accepted. But since these feelings were too extreme/unbearable for you, you had to repress them as a child.

In times of emotional overload or when we were forbidden to show certain feelings, a protective mechanism took place: we repressed these feelings from our consciousness. However, they remain stored in us and come up again and again. Mostly they are triggered by seemingly quite banal situations (= "triggered").

This questionnaire was created after years of healing my childhood suppressed emotions, which kept coming to the surface. A trivial comment, an unpleasant situation in everyday life, a wry look. And suddenly I was seized by violent feelings. Little by little, however, I was able to deal with them more and more consciously, and out of this came those questions that helped me the most to reintegrate and heal the feelings that had once been cut off. I would now like to give you these questions. Every time something triggers you emotionally, you can take the questionnaire in a safe place and "park" your feelings there. Notice them and give them space and room to show themselves, to speak and to be held. No one used to explain to us how to deal with such strong emotions. No one told us how do I not drown or suffocate in sadness, burn up from my anger, or survive the rigidity of my fainting.

This was very overwhelming and therefore we found emergency strategies to be able to endure these enormous tensions within us. We took refuge in rushes, addictions, superficial conversations and even self-injurious measures to avoid feeling all this. Unconsciously. Not knowing that there is also a healthy way: To feel these feelings, to give them space, to integrate them. To see them, to hear them, to feel them.

We can now catch up with this whenever the emotions acutely surface. A situation that triggers those emotions is even a gift, as it can reveal great healing when properly unpacked. For this very purpose, you will now receive a questionnaire that you can fill out every time you feel emotionally bad after old pain triggering situations. The first questionnaire is a sample questionnaire already filled out for easier understanding.

Questions 7 and 8 are about being there mentally for the hurt part of you. I have tried to illustrate this best with the example, as there is hardly a blanket guide for this. Follow your heart and give these younger "I's" of yours all that they need right now (listening, being seen, acknowledging their feelings, being held, loving people it trusts, understanding, a warm blanket or stuffed animal/toy, a change of space, a change of the painful situation for the better. This is very individual. You can trust your present spiritual strength to send you the right impulses. And if you find this difficult, it's okay, because after all you have already noticed your feelings before, which is such an infinitely valuable step.

Whenever something triggers you emotionally, you can take the questionnaires and write down your feelings there, look at them and give them space to show themselves.
Give them a hearing and loving attention. After each questionnaire, there is a page for your own notes and space to express your feelings in a frame.
Fill the frame with whatever your emotions are trying to get rid of. No matter what. You can smear around full of anger or draw fine lines full of sadness or whatever "wants to come out".

In order to be able to open up to these questions, it is first necessary to deal with the fear of feelings, if you close yourself off completely from feelings.

For example, for a long time I was afraid to even allow the emotion of anger because I thought that this anger in me was destructive, could hurt people, or that the new aliveness could confuse others.

The fear kept me from being able to give space to the anger.

Therefore, first answer the following questions:

1. fear immediately arises at the idea of feeling any emotion inside me and acting it out:

O yes O no

2. fear immediately arises at the idea of feeling and acting out anger inside me:

O yes O no

3. fear immediately arises at the idea of feeling sadness inside me:

O yes O no

4. fear immediately arises at the idea of feeling powerlessness and helplessness in me:

O yes O no

5. fear immediately arises at the idea of feeling joy in me and expressing it:

O yes O no

If you answered "yes" to any question, first fill out the following questionnaire:

Fear

1. Where in the body can you feel the fear? Just perceive it.

_____

2. How big is it, what shape and color is it?

_____

3. What does she want to tell you, what words spontaneously come to your mind when you perceive her?

_____

_____

_____

4. Can she answer the question why she is afraid of this one feeling or all feelings?

_____

_____

_____

5. What do you notice she might need right now?
Does she just want to be allowed to be there, to be held, felt and understood or does she need something very specific?

_____

_____

_____

6. Can you give her this? (it will also do mentally)
O yes O no

_____

_____

7. is she changing? Is the anxiety getting smaller?
O yes O no

If no, try again at another time to feel it and give it space.

If yes, you can now always take the following trigger questionnaire in a difficult situation that triggers very strong feelings. Answer as many questions as possible. For example, if you don't see any color, it doesn't matter.
The main thing is that you give space to the feelings inside you.

The healing forces of life keep bringing

you into situations similar to those in

which you were hurt.

Until you are ready to let go of

the misunderstanding that was

created then.

- Veit Lindau

All the misunderstandings now
get the opportunity to reveal their
truth and transform their inherent

painful feelings

Trigger Questionnaire

- completed example -

1. What just happened?

The bakery saleswoman made it clear to me in a severe tone that it was not yet my turn to order. This hit something inside me and I was suddenly very scared and fled to the car.

2. What are you feeling right now?

○ anger ○ sadness ○ powerlessness ⊗ **fear** ○ shame ○ stress ○ despair ○ heaviness ○ emptiness ○ indefinable

other feeling: _____

3. Where is this feeling in the body?

○ neck ○ chest ○ stomach ○ arms ○ legs ○ back ○ head ○ shoulders
⊗ **everywhere**
⊗ elsewhere: **all around me**

4. What color is it in your mind's eye:

⊗ Yellow ○ Blue ○ Red ○ Green ○ Black ○ Grey ○ Purple x White ○ Pink
○ Brown ○ Colorful ⊗ other color : **Yellow-white mixed**

5. What shape or form is it:

⊗ **distorted** ○ round ball ○ constricting object ○ stone ○ water ○ fire ○ splinter ○ lightning ○ cloud ○ smoke ○ bubble ○ abyss ○ hole ○ sandstorm ○ volcanic eruption ○ fog ○ pinpricks ○ crater ○ flames ○ constricting coat
⊗ other form: *like a distorted veil enveloping me*

6. Does the feeling want to do something or act out ? If yes, do it with pleasure.

○ punch a pillow ○ shake myself ○ scream ○ draw or write something ⊗ **pull a blanket over my head** ○ yawn

⊗ something else: *run away, hide*

7. Does it want to tell you something or do words appear inside you?

What has this feeling always wanted to say and get rid of?:

I'm so afraid of doing something wrong again. To be punished or beaten for it again. I always have the feeling that I am treading on eggshells that I must not break. I do nothing right. Always everything wrong wrong wrong. When will this finally stop. Will me crawl away and rest from the world in which one constantly does something wrong.

♡ I hold this side in me, understand it, talk to it, take it seriously ♡

She has suffered so much and was locked in a basement room for mistakes. I take her in my arms and show understanding for her feelings. "Of course you're scared, that's very clear. It is very unfair what is happening to you and how you are being treated. There are no mistakes, and certainly not such trivial "mistakes" that you are accused of. You are always right and everything you do is fine. I am with you now and help you. You are never alone anymore and always protected by me. I love you very much."

8. Do pictures and/or memories come up?

○ no → continue with question 9

⊗ **yes, mentally go into them:**

I see in my mind's eye the dark basement room with a lot of wood in it and only a small window on the ceiling. The child sitting there is confused and does not know what is happening to him. It is making fun of its father, who has locked it in because of a small mishap. He is trying to suppress his true feelings by laughing. I observe the situation and relive it. I feel the stuffy air and the stifling darkness. The confusion and fear of further "mistakes" and punishment.

The fear is allowed to be fully there, I feel it all over my body. Now I imagine the child being rescued from the basement room by a dear friend of the parents, who often looked after the child at the time. She carries the child up, into the warm sunlight and gives him his favorite stuffed animal. The child is held and feels protected.

At times I observe the situation, and at times I am one with the child. My consciousness slides into different perspectives of this situation and the healing that is now taking place.

9. Do you feel anything different now from what you felt in question 2?

○ disappointment ○ envy ○ anger ⊗ **sadness** ○ boredom ○ frustration ○ joy
○ despair ○ helplessness x neutral
⊗ other feeling: *a little sad and relieved*

Do you find understanding for your feelings? For example, maybe you were really just disappointed, and angry as a result?

I was very afraid of making mistakes, but was actually also very sad that I could never please my father, whom I loved very much.

10. Do you now see the situation that happened in question 1 with different eyes? How would you describe it neutrally?

Looking at it neutrally, I simply went into a bakery and ordered something, although someone else was still being served.

Maybe the saleswoman had already had a stressful day and was therefore a bit annoyed by my hasty order. The situation was not bad at all.

11. What would Love say to you now? Answer spontaneously ♡

There is no "right" and "wrong." Everything is ok and you will always do the right thing, no matter if you fall down with it or not. Everything is for an experience. Once we fall down, we just get back up.
So "mistakes" don't exist at all. You are always safe, nothing can happen to you.

12. If you are also open to spiritual things:

Ask inwardly for spiritual help and just be open to what comes.

You perceive: ○ loving, gentle, quiet words ⊗ **a subtle, touching energy**

○ colors that envelop and strengthen you ○ a basic trust in life ⊗ **protective, invisible embrace**

○ something else: _____

13. Is there anything you intuitively would like to do right now from your heart? If yes, do it very much ☺

a spontaneous meeting with a friend in nature would do me good now

Space for notes, words or pictures that want to express your feelings:

I am ashamed of my reaction (the escape from the bakery).
But the fear was there and therefore I could not help it.
The fear seems so big and overpowering. It's hard to feel it
consciously, but if I just notice it, it changes and becomes
smaller. I imagine myself just standing next to it and looking at
that yellow and white color.
She's just there. And dissolving more and more. The fear also
says it wants to protect me and why I want to make it go away.
She just wants to help me. I thank her and give her space.

On the following pages you will find the Trigger Questionnaire, which you can fill out whenever you are triggered.

If possible, take it immediately when the emotion is still tangible.

I wish you deep healing and great insights.

Trigger Questionnaire

1. What just happened?

_____

_____

_____

2. What are you feeling right now?

○ anger ○ sadness ○ powerlessness ○ fear ○ shame ○ stress

○ despair ○ heaviness ○ emptiness ○ indefinable

○ **other feeling:** _____

3. Where is this feeling in the body?

○ neck ○ chest ○ stomach ○ arms ○ legs ○ back

○ head ○ shoulders

○ **anywhere else:** _____

4. What color is it in your mind's eye:

○ yellow ○ blue ○ red ○ green ○ black ○ gray ○ purple

○ white ○ pink ○ brown ○ colorful

○ **other color :** _____

5. What shape or form does it have:

○ distorted ○ round ball ○ constricting object ○ stone ○ water

○ fire ○ splinters ○ lightning ○ cloud ○ smoke ○ bubble ○ abyss ○ hole ○

sandstorm ○ volcanic eruption ○ fog ○ pinpricks ○ crater ○ flames

○ constricting mantle ○ **other form:** _____

6. Does the feeling want to do something or act out ? If so, feel free to do it.

○ punch a pillow ○ shake yourself ○ scream ○ draw or write something ○ pull a blanket over your head ○ yawn ○ **something else:** _____

7. **Does it want to tell you something or do words appear inside you? What has this feeling always wanted to say and get rid of?:**

_____

_____

♡ *Take a moment and hold this side of you, understand it, talk to it, take it seriously* ♡

8. **Do images and/or memories come up?**

○ no → continue with question 9

○ yes → go into them mentally:

Consider the environment of the situation, relive the memory as an observer, acknowledge the emotions at the time, intuitively change the memory positively, e.g. with the help of an adult.

9. **Do you feel anything different now than you did in question 2?**

○ disappointment ○ envy ○ anger ○ sadness ○ boredom

○ frustration ○ joy ○ despair ○ helplessness ○ neutral

○ other feeling: _____

Do you find understanding for your feelings? For example, maybe you were really just disappointed, and angry as a result? Or just angry about something that caused you to feel powerless?

_____

_____

10. Do you now see the situation that happened in question 1 with different eyes? How would you describe it in neutral terms?

_____

_____

_____

11. What would Love say to you now? Answer spontaneously ♡

_____

_____

_____

_____

12. If you are also open to spiritual things:
Ask inwardly for spiritual help and just be open to what comes.

You perceive: ○ loving, gentle, quiet words ○ a subtle, touching energy ○ colors that envelop and strengthen you ○ peaceful mood ○ a mental image of light-filled helpers who are simply there ○ golden light flowing into your heart ○ a basic trust in life ○ protective, invisible embrace

○ something else: _____

13. Is there anything you intuitively would like to do right now from your heart? If so, do it very much :)

○ talk to a good friend ○ go to nature ○ drink a tea ○ take a bath ○ clarify a situation from a new, clear perspective ○ be creative ○ do a hobby ○ light exercise ○ listen to music ○ just relax ○ hug yourself ○ be grateful for this healing experience

○ something else: _____

Space for notes, words or pictures that want to express your feelings:

_____

_____

_____

_____

_____

_____

_____

_____

Trigger Questionnaire

1. What just happened?

_____

_____

_____

2. What are you feeling right now?

○ anger ○ sadness ○ powerlessness ○ fear ○ shame ○ stress

○ despair ○ heaviness ○ emptiness ○ indefinable

○ **other feeling:** _____

3. Where is this feeling in the body?

○ neck ○ chest ○ stomach ○ arms ○ legs ○ back

○ head ○ shoulders

○ **anywhere else:** _____

4. What color is it in your mind's eye:

○ yellow ○ blue ○ red ○ green ○ black ○ gray ○ purple

○ white ○ pink ○ brown ○ colorful

○ **other color :** _____

5. What shape or form does it have:

○ distorted ○ round ball ○ constricting object ○ stone ○ water

○ fire ○ splinters ○ lightning ○ cloud ○ smoke ○ bubble ○ abyss ○ hole ○

sandstorm ○ volcanic eruption ○ fog ○ pinpricks ○ crater ○ flames

○ constricting mantle ○ **other form:** _____

6. Does the feeling want to do something or act out ? If so, feel free to do it.

○ punch a pillow ○ shake yourself ○ scream ○ draw or write something ○ pull a blanket over your head ○ yawn ○ **something else:** _____

7. **Does it want to tell you something or do words appear inside you? What has this feeling always wanted to say and get rid of?:**

_____

_____

♡ *Take a moment and hold this side of you, understand it, talk to it, take it seriously* ♡

8. **Do images and/or memories come up?**

○ no → continue with question 9

○ yes → go into them mentally:

Consider the environment of the situation, relive the memory as an observer, acknowledge the emotions at the time, intuitively change the memory positively, e.g. with the help of an adult.

9. **Do you feel anything different now than you did in question 2?**

○ disappointment ○ envy ○ anger ○ sadness ○ boredom

○ frustration ○ joy ○ despair ○ helplessness ○ neutral

○ other feeling: _____

Do you find understanding for your feelings? For example, maybe you were really just disappointed, and angry as a result? Or just angry about something that caused you to feel powerless?

_____

_____

10. Do you now see the situation that happened in question 1 with different eyes? How would you describe it in neutral terms?

_____

_____

_____

11. What would Love say to you now? Answer spontaneously ♡

_____

_____

_____

_____

12. If you are also open to spiritual things:

Ask inwardly for spiritual help and just be open to what comes.

You perceive: ○ loving, gentle, quiet words ○ a subtle, touching energy ○ colors that envelop and strengthen you ○ peaceful mood ○ a mental image of light-filled helpers who are simply there ○ golden light flowing into your heart ○ a basic trust in life ○ protective, invisible embrace

○ **something else:** _____

13. Is there anything you intuitively would like to do right now from your heart? If so, do it very much :)

○ talk to a good friend ○ go to nature ○ drink a tea ○ take a bath ○ clarify a situation from a new, clear perspective ○ be creative ○ do a hobby ○ light exercise ○ listen to music ○ just relax ○ hug yourself ○ be grateful for this healing experience

○ **something else:** _____

Space for notes, words or pictures that want to express your feelings:

_____

_____

_____

_____

_____

_____

_____

_____

Trigger Questionnaire

1. What just happened?

_____

_____

_____

2. What are you feeling right now?

○ anger ○ sadness ○ powerlessness ○ fear ○ shame ○ stress

○ despair ○ heaviness ○ emptiness ○ indefinable

○ **other feeling:** _____

3. Where is this feeling in the body?

○ neck ○ chest ○ stomach ○ arms ○ legs ○ back

○ head ○ shoulders

○ **anywhere else:** _____

4. What color is it in your mind's eye:

○ yellow ○ blue ○ red ○ green ○ black ○ gray ○ purple

○ white ○ pink ○ brown ○ colorful

○ **other color :** _____

5. What shape or form does it have:

○ distorted ○ round ball ○ constricting object ○ stone ○ water

○ fire ○ splinters ○ lightning ○ cloud ○ smoke ○ bubble ○ abyss ○ hole ○

sandstorm ○ volcanic eruption ○ fog ○ pinpricks ○ crater ○ flames

○ constricting mantle ○ **other form:** _____

6. Does the feeling want to do something or act out ? If so, feel free to do
t.

○ punch a pillow ○ shake yourself ○ scream ○ draw or write something ○
pull a blanket over your head ○ yawn ○ **something else:** _____

7. **Does it want to tell you something or do words appear inside you?**
What has this feeling always wanted to say and get rid of?:

_____

_____

♡ *Take a moment and hold this side of you, understand it, talk to it, take it*

seriously ♡

8. **Do images and/or memories come up?**

○ no → continue with question 9

○ yes → go into them mentally:
Consider the environment of the situation, relive the memory as an observer,
acknowledge the emotions at the time, intuitively change the memory
positively, e.g. with the help of an adult.

9. **Do you feel anything different now than you did in question 2?**

○ disappointment ○ envy ○ anger ○ sadness ○ boredom

○ frustration ○ joy ○ despair ○ helplessness ○ neutral

○ other feeling: _____

Do you find understanding for your feelings? For example, maybe you were really
just disappointed, and angry as a result? Or just angry about something that caused
you to feel powerless?

_____

_____

10. Do you now see the situation that happened in question 1 with different eyes? How would you describe it in neutral terms?

_____

_____

_____

11. What would Love say to you now? Answer spontaneously ♡

_____

_____

_____

_____

12. If you are also open to spiritual things:
Ask inwardly for spiritual help and just be open to what comes.
You perceive: ○ loving, gentle, quiet words ○ a subtle, touching energy ○ colors that envelop and strengthen you ○ peaceful mood ○ a mental image of light-filled helpers who are simply there ○ golden light flowing into your heart ○ a basic trust in life ○ protective, invisible embrace
○ something else: _____

13. Is there anything you intuitively would like to do right now from your heart? If so, do it very much :)
○ talk to a good friend ○ go to nature ○ drink a tea ○ take a bath ○ clarify a situation from a new, clear perspective ○ be creative ○ do a hobby ○ light exercise ○ listen to music ○ just relax ○ hug yourself ○ be grateful for this healing experience
○ something else: _____

Space for notes, words or pictures that want to express your feelings:

_____

_____

_____

_____

_____

_____

_____

Trigger Questionnaire

1. What just happened?

_____

_____

_____

2. What are you feeling right now?

○ anger ○ sadness ○ powerlessness ○ fear ○ shame ○ stress

○ despair ○ heaviness ○ emptiness ○ indefinable

○ **other feeling:** _____

3. Where is this feeling in the body?

○ neck ○ chest ○ stomach ○ arms ○ legs ○ back

○ head ○ shoulders

○ **anywhere else:** _____

4. What color is it in your mind's eye:

○ yellow ○ blue ○ red ○ green ○ black ○ gray ○ purple

○ white ○ pink ○ brown ○ colorful

○ **other color :** _____

5. What shape or form does it have:

○ distorted ○ round ball ○ constricting object ○ stone ○ water

○ fire ○ splinters ○ lightning ○ cloud ○ smoke ○ bubble ○ abyss ○ hole ○

sandstorm ○ volcanic eruption ○ fog ○ pinpricks ○ crater ○ flames

○ constricting mantle ○ **other form:** _____

6. Does the feeling want to do something or act out ? If so, feel free to do it.

○ punch a pillow ○ shake yourself ○ scream ○ draw or write something ○ pull a blanket over your head ○ yawn ○ **something else:** _____

7. Does it want to tell you something or do words appear inside you? What has this feeling always wanted to say and get rid of?:

_____

_____

♡ *Take a moment and hold this side of you, understand it, talk to it, take it seriously* ♡

8. Do images and/or memories come up?

○ no → continue with question 9

○ yes → go into them mentally:

Consider the environment of the situation, relive the memory as an observer, acknowledge the emotions at the time, intuitively change the memory positively, e.g. with the help of an adult.

9. Do you feel anything different now than you did in question 2?

○ disappointment ○ envy ○ anger ○ sadness ○ boredom

○ frustration ○ joy ○ despair ○ helplessness ○ neutral

○ other feeling: _____

Do you find understanding for your feelings? For example, maybe you were really just disappointed, and angry as a result? Or just angry about something that caused you to feel powerless?

_____

_____

10. Do you now see the situation that happened in question 1 with different eyes? How would you describe it in neutral terms?

_____

_____

_____

11. What would Love say to you now? Answer spontaneously ♡

_____

_____

_____

_____

12. If you are also open to spiritual things:

Ask inwardly for spiritual help and just be open to what comes.

You perceive: ○ loving, gentle, quiet words ○ a subtle, touching energy ○ colors that envelop and strengthen you ○ peaceful mood ○ a mental image of light-filled helpers who are simply there ○ golden light flowing into your heart ○ a basic trust in life ○ protective, invisible embrace

○ **something else:** _____

13. Is there anything you intuitively would like to do right now from your heart? If so, do it very much :)

○ talk to a good friend ○ go to nature ○ drink a tea ○ take a bath ○ clarify a situation from a new, clear perspective ○ be creative ○ do a hobby ○ light exercise ○ listen to music ○ just relax ○ hug yourself ○ be grateful for this healing experience

○ **something else:** _____

Space for notes, words or pictures that want to express your feelings:

_____

_____

_____

_____

_____

_____

_____

_____

Trigger Questionnaire

1. What just happened?

_____

_____

_____

2. What are you feeling right now?

○ anger ○ sadness ○ powerlessness ○ fear ○ shame ○ stress

○ despair ○ heaviness ○ emptiness ○ indefinable

○ **other feeling:** _____

3. Where is this feeling in the body?

○ neck ○ chest ○ stomach ○ arms ○ legs ○ back

○ head ○ shoulders

○ **anywhere else:** _____

4. What color is it in your mind's eye:

○ yellow ○ blue ○ red ○ green ○ black ○ gray ○ purple

○ white ○ pink ○ brown ○ colorful

○ **other color :** _____

5. What shape or form does it have:

○ distorted ○ round ball ○ constricting object ○ stone ○ water

○ fire ○ splinters ○ lightning ○ cloud ○ smoke ○ bubble ○ abyss ○ hole ○

sandstorm ○ volcanic eruption ○ fog ○ pinpricks ○ crater ○ flames

○ constricting mantle ○ **other form:** _____

6. Does the feeling want to do something or act out ? If so, feel free to do it.

○ punch a pillow ○ shake yourself ○ scream ○ draw or write something ○ pull a blanket over your head ○ yawn ○ **something else:** _____

7. Does it want to tell you something or do words appear inside you? What has this feeling always wanted to say and get rid of?:

_____

_____

♡ *Take a moment and hold this side of you, understand it, talk to it, take it seriously* ♡

8. Do images and/or memories come up?

○ no → continue with question 9

○ yes → go into them mentally:

Consider the environment of the situation, relive the memory as an observer, acknowledge the emotions at the time, intuitively change the memory positively, e.g. with the help of an adult.

9. Do you feel anything different now than you did in question 2?

○ disappointment ○ envy ○ anger ○ sadness ○ boredom

○ frustration ○ joy ○ despair ○ helplessness ○ neutral

○ other feeling: _____

Do you find understanding for your feelings? For example, maybe you were really just disappointed, and angry as a result? Or just angry about something that caused you to feel powerless?

_____

_____

10. Do you now see the situation that happened in question 1 with different eyes? How would you describe it in neutral terms?

_____

_____

_____

11. What would Love say to you now? Answer spontaneously ♡

_____

_____

_____

_____

12. If you are also open to spiritual things:
Ask inwardly for spiritual help and just be open to what comes.
You perceive: ○ loving, gentle, quiet words ○ a subtle, touching energy ○ colors that envelop and strengthen you ○ peaceful mood ○ a mental image of light-filled helpers who are simply there ○ golden light flowing into your heart ○ a basic trust in life ○ protective, invisible embrace
○ something else: _____

13. Is there anything you intuitively would like to do right now from your heart? If so, do it very much :)
○ talk to a good friend ○ go to nature ○ drink a tea ○ take a bath ○ clarify a situation from a new, clear perspective ○ be creative ○ do a hobby ○ light exercise ○ listen to music ○ just relax ○ hug yourself ○ be grateful for this healing experience
○ something else: _____

Space for notes, words or pictures that want to express your feelings:

_____

_____

_____

_____

_____

_____

_____

Trigger Questionnaire

1. What just happened?

_____

_____

_____

2. What are you feeling right now?

○ anger ○ sadness ○ powerlessness ○ fear ○ shame ○ stress

○ despair ○ heaviness ○ emptiness ○ indefinable

○ **other feeling:** _____

3. Where is this feeling in the body?

○ neck ○ chest ○ stomach ○ arms ○ legs ○ back

○ head ○ shoulders

○ **anywhere else:** _____

4. What color is it in your mind's eye:

○ yellow ○ blue ○ red ○ green ○ black ○ gray ○ purple

○ white ○ pink ○ brown ○ colorful

○ **other color :** _____

5. What shape or form does it have:

○ distorted ○ round ball ○ constricting object ○ stone ○ water

○ fire ○ splinters ○ lightning ○ cloud ○ smoke ○ bubble ○ abyss ○ hole ○

sandstorm ○ volcanic eruption ○ fog ○ pinpricks ○ crater ○ flames

○ constricting mantle ○ **other form:** _____

6. Does the feeling want to do something or act out ? If so, feel free to do it.

○ punch a pillow ○ shake yourself ○ scream ○ draw or write something ○ pull a blanket over your head ○ yawn ○ **something else:** _____

7. **Does it want to tell you something or do words appear inside you? What has this feeling always wanted to say and get rid of?:**

_____

_____

♡ *Take a moment and hold this side of you, understand it, talk to it, take it seriously* ♡

8. **Do images and/or memories come up?**

○ no → continue with question 9

○ yes → go into them mentally:

Consider the environment of the situation, relive the memory as an observer, acknowledge the emotions at the time, intuitively change the memory positively, e.g. with the help of an adult.

9. **Do you feel anything different now than you did in question 2?**

○ disappointment ○ envy ○ anger ○ sadness ○ boredom

○ frustration ○ joy ○ despair ○ helplessness ○ neutral

○ other feeling: _____

Do you find understanding for your feelings? For example, maybe you were really just disappointed, and angry as a result? Or just angry about something that caused you to feel powerless?

_____

_____

10. Do you now see the situation that happened in question 1 with different eyes? How would you describe it in neutral terms?

_____

_____

_____

11. What would Love say to you now? Answer spontaneously ♡

_____

_____

_____

_____

12. If you are also open to spiritual things:
Ask inwardly for spiritual help and just be open to what comes.

You perceive: ○ loving, gentle, quiet words ○ a subtle, touching energy ○ colors that envelop and strengthen you ○ peaceful mood ○ a mental image of light-filled helpers who are simply there ○ golden light flowing into your heart ○ a basic trust in life ○ protective, invisible embrace

○ **something else:** _____

13. Is there anything you intuitively would like to do right now from your heart? If so, do it very much :)

○ talk to a good friend ○ go to nature ○ drink a tea ○ take a bath ○ clarify a situation from a new, clear perspective ○ be creative ○ do a hobby ○ light exercise ○ listen to music ○ just relax ○ hug yourself ○ be grateful for this healing experience

○ **something else:** _____

Space for notes, words or pictures that want to express your feelings:

_____

_____

_____

_____

_____

_____

_____

_____

Trigger Questionnaire

1. What just happened?

_____

_____

_____

2. What are you feeling right now?

○ anger ○ sadness ○ powerlessness ○ fear ○ shame ○ stress

○ despair ○ heaviness ○ emptiness ○ indefinable

○ **other feeling:** _____

3. Where is this feeling in the body?

○ neck ○ chest ○ stomach ○ arms ○ legs ○ back

○ head ○ shoulders

○ **anywhere else:** _____

4. What color is it in your mind's eye:

○ yellow ○ blue ○ red ○ green ○ black ○ gray ○ purple

○ white ○ pink ○ brown ○ colorful

○ **other color :** _____

5. What shape or form does it have:

○ distorted ○ round ball ○ constricting object ○ stone ○ water

○ fire ○ splinters ○ lightning ○ cloud ○ smoke ○ bubble ○ abyss ○ hole ○

sandstorm ○ volcanic eruption ○ fog ○ pinpricks ○ crater ○ flames

○ constricting mantle ○ **other form:** _____

6. Does the feeling want to do something or act out ? If so, feel free to do
it.

○ punch a pillow ○ shake yourself ○ scream ○ draw or write something ○
pull a blanket over your head ○ yawn ○ **something else:** _____

7. Does it want to tell you something or do words appear inside you?
What has this feeling always wanted to say and get rid of?:

_____

_____

♡ *Take a moment and hold this side of you, understand it, talk to it, take it*

seriously ♡

8. Do images and/or memories come up?

○ no → continue with question 9

○ yes → go into them mentally:

Consider the environment of the situation, relive the memory as an observer,
acknowledge the emotions at the time, intuitively change the memory
positively, e.g. with the help of an adult.

9. Do you feel anything different now than you did in question 2?

○ disappointment ○ envy ○ anger ○ sadness ○ boredom

○ frustration ○ joy ○ despair ○ helplessness ○ neutral

○ other feeling: _____

Do you find understanding for your feelings? For example, maybe you were really
just disappointed, and angry as a result? Or just angry about something that caused
you to feel powerless?

_____

_____

10. Do you now see the situation that happened in question 1 with different eyes? How would you describe it in neutral terms?

_____

_____

_____

11. What would Love say to you now? Answer spontaneously ♡

_____

_____

_____

_____

12. If you are also open to spiritual things:
Ask inwardly for spiritual help and just be open to what comes.

You perceive: ○ loving, gentle, quiet words ○ a subtle, touching energy ○ colors that envelop and strengthen you ○ peaceful mood ○ a mental image of light-filled helpers who are simply there ○ golden light flowing into your heart ○ a basic trust in life ○ protective, invisible embrace

○ something else: _____

13. Is there anything you intuitively would like to do right now from your heart? If so, do it very much :)

○ talk to a good friend ○ go to nature ○ drink a tea ○ take a bath ○ clarify a situation from a new, clear perspective ○ be creative ○ do a hobby ○ light exercise ○ listen to music ○ just relax ○ hug yourself ○ be grateful for this healing experience

○ something else: _____

Space for notes, words or pictures that want to express your feelings:

_____

_____

_____

_____

_____

_____

_____

_____

Trigger Questionnaire

1. What just happened?

_____

_____

_____

2. What are you feeling right now?

○ anger ○ sadness ○ powerlessness ○ fear ○ shame ○ stress

○ despair ○ heaviness ○ emptiness ○ indefinable

○ **other feeling:** _____

3. Where is this feeling in the body?

○ neck ○ chest ○ stomach ○ arms ○ legs ○ back

○ head ○ shoulders

○ **anywhere else:** _____

4. What color is it in your mind's eye:

○ yellow ○ blue ○ red ○ green ○ black ○ gray ○ purple

○ white ○ pink ○ brown ○ colorful

○ **other color :** _____

5. What shape or form does it have:

○ distorted ○ round ball ○ constricting object ○ stone ○ water

○ fire ○ splinters ○ lightning ○ cloud ○ smoke ○ bubble ○ abyss ○ hole ○

sandstorm ○ volcanic eruption ○ fog ○ pinpricks ○ crater ○ flames

○ constricting mantle ○ **other form:** _____

. Does the feeling want to do something or act out ? If so, feel free to do
t.

⊃ punch a pillow ○ shake yourself ○ scream ○ draw or write something ○
pull a blanket over your head ○ yawn ○ **something else:** _____

7. Does it want to tell you something or do words appear inside you?
What has this feeling always wanted to say and get rid of?:
_____
_____

♡ *Take a moment and hold this side of you, understand it, talk to it, take it*
seriously ♡

8. Do images and/or memories come up?
○ no → continue with question 9
○ yes → go into them mentally:
Consider the environment of the situation, relive the memory as an observer,
acknowledge the emotions at the time, intuitively change the memory
positively, e.g. with the help of an adult.

9. Do you feel anything different now than you did in question 2?
○ disappointment ○ envy ○ anger ○ sadness ○ boredom
○ frustration ○ joy ○ despair ○ helplessness ○ neutral
○ other feeling: _____
Do you find understanding for your feelings? For example, maybe you were really
just disappointed, and angry as a result? Or just angry about something that caused
you to feel powerless?
_____
_____

10. Do you now see the situation that happened in question 1 with different eyes? How would you describe it in neutral terms?

_____

_____

_____

11. What would Love say to you now? Answer spontaneously ♡

_____

_____

_____

_____

12. If you are also open to spiritual things:
Ask inwardly for spiritual help and just be open to what comes.

You perceive: ○ loving, gentle, quiet words ○ a subtle, touching energy ○ colors that envelop and strengthen you ○ peaceful mood ○ a mental image of light-filled helpers who are simply there ○ golden light flowing into your heart ○ a basic trust in life ○ protective, invisible embrace

○ something else: _____

13. Is there anything you intuitively would like to do right now from your heart? If so, do it very much :)

○ talk to a good friend ○ go to nature ○ drink a tea ○ take a bath ○ clarify a situation from a new, clear perspective ○ be creative ○ do a hobby ○ light exercise ○ listen to music ○ just relax ○ hug yourself ○ be grateful for this healing experience

○ something else: _____

Space for notes, words or pictures that want to express your feelings:

_____

_____

_____

_____

_____

_____

_____

Trigger Questionnaire

1. What just happened?

_____

_____

_____

2. What are you feeling right now?

○ anger ○ sadness ○ powerlessness ○ fear ○ shame ○ stress

○ despair ○ heaviness ○ emptiness ○ indefinable

○ **other feeling:** _____

3. Where is this feeling in the body?

○ neck ○ chest ○ stomach ○ arms ○ legs ○ back

○ head ○ shoulders

○ **anywhere else:** _____

4. What color is it in your mind's eye:

○ yellow ○ blue ○ red ○ green ○ black ○ gray ○ purple

○ white ○ pink ○ brown ○ colorful

○ **other color :** _____

5. What shape or form does it have:

○ distorted ○ round ball ○ constricting object ○ stone ○ water

○ fire ○ splinters ○ lightning ○ cloud ○ smoke ○ bubble ○ abyss ○ hole ○

sandstorm ○ volcanic eruption ○ fog ○ pinpricks ○ crater ○ flames

○ constricting mantle ○ **other form:** _____

. Does the feeling want to do something or act out ? If so, feel free to do
t.

○ punch a pillow ○ shake yourself ○ scream ○ draw or write something ○
pull a blanket over your head ○ yawn ○ **something else:** _____

7. Does it want to tell you something or do words appear inside you?
What has this feeling always wanted to say and get rid of?:

_____

_____

♡ *Take a moment and hold this side of you, understand it, talk to it, take it*

seriously ♡

8. Do images and/or memories come up?

○ no → continue with question 9

○ yes → go into them mentally:
Consider the environment of the situation, relive the memory as an observer,
acknowledge the emotions at the time, intuitively change the memory
positively, e.g. with the help of an adult.

9. Do you feel anything different now than you did in question 2?

○ disappointment ○ envy ○ anger ○ sadness ○ boredom

○ frustration ○ joy ○ despair ○ helplessness ○ neutral

○ other feeling: _____

Do you find understanding for your feelings? For example, maybe you were really
just disappointed, and angry as a result? Or just angry about something that caused
you to feel powerless?

_____

_____

10. Do you now see the situation that happened in question 1 with different eyes? How would you describe it in neutral terms?

_____

_____

_____

11. What would Love say to you now? Answer spontaneously ♡

_____

_____

_____

_____

12. If you are also open to spiritual things:

Ask inwardly for spiritual help and just be open to what comes.

You perceive: ○ loving, gentle, quiet words ○ a subtle, touching energy ○ colors that envelop and strengthen you ○ peaceful mood ○ a mental image of light-filled helpers who are simply there ○ golden light flowing into your heart ○ a basic trust in life ○ protective, invisible embrace

○ something else: _____

13. Is there anything you intuitively would like to do right now from your heart? If so, do it very much :)

○ talk to a good friend ○ go to nature ○ drink a tea ○ take a bath ○ clarify a situation from a new, clear perspective ○ be creative ○ do a hobby ○ light exercise ○ listen to music ○ just relax ○ hug yourself ○ be grateful for this healing experience

○ something else: _____

Space for notes, words or pictures that want to express your feelings:

_____

_____

_____

_____

_____

_____

_____

Trigger Questionnaire

1. What just happened?

_____

_____

_____

2. What are you feeling right now?

○ anger ○ sadness ○ powerlessness ○ fear ○ shame ○ stress

○ despair ○ heaviness ○ emptiness ○ indefinable

○ **other feeling:** _____

3. Where is this feeling in the body?

○ neck ○ chest ○ stomach ○ arms ○ legs ○ back

○ head ○ shoulders

○ **anywhere else:** _____

4. What color is it in your mind's eye:

○ yellow ○ blue ○ red ○ green ○ black ○ gray ○ purple

○ white ○ pink ○ brown ○ colorful

○ **other color :** _____

5. What shape or form does it have:

○ distorted ○ round ball ○ constricting object ○ stone ○ water

○ fire ○ splinters ○ lightning ○ cloud ○ smoke ○ bubble ○ abyss ○ hole ○

sandstorm ○ volcanic eruption ○ fog ○ pinpricks ○ crater ○ flames

○ constricting mantle ○ **other form:** _____

. Does the feeling want to do something or act out ? If so, feel free to do
t.

◯ punch a pillow ◯ shake yourself ◯ scream ◯ draw or write something ◯
pull a blanket over your head ◯ yawn ◯ **something else:** _____

7. Does it want to tell you something or do words appear inside you?
What has this feeling always wanted to say and get rid of?:

_____

_____

♡ *Take a moment and hold this side of you, understand it, talk to it, take it*

seriously ♡

8. Do images and/or memories come up?

◯ no → continue with question 9

◯ yes → go into them mentally:
Consider the environment of the situation, relive the memory as an observer,
acknowledge the emotions at the time, intuitively change the memory
positively, e.g. with the help of an adult.

9. Do you feel anything different now than you did in question 2?

◯ disappointment ◯ envy ◯ anger ◯ sadness ◯ boredom

◯ frustration ◯ joy ◯ despair ◯ helplessness ◯ neutral

◯ other feeling: _____

Do you find understanding for your feelings? For example, maybe you were really
just disappointed, and angry as a result? Or just angry about something that caused
you to feel powerless?

_____

_____

10. Do you now see the situation that happened in question 1 with different eyes? How would you describe it in neutral terms?

_____

_____

_____

11. What would Love say to you now? Answer spontaneously ♡

_____

_____

_____

_____

12. If you are also open to spiritual things:
Ask inwardly for spiritual help and just be open to what comes.
You perceive: ○ loving, gentle, quiet words ○ a subtle, touching energy ○ colors that envelop and strengthen you ○ peaceful mood ○ a mental image of light-filled helpers who are simply there ○ golden light flowing into your heart ○ a basic trust in life ○ protective, invisible embrace
○ something else: _____

13. Is there anything you intuitively would like to do right now from your heart? If so, do it very much :)
○ talk to a good friend ○ go to nature ○ drink a tea ○ take a bath ○ clarify a situation from a new, clear perspective ○ be creative ○ do a hobby ○ light exercise ○ listen to music ○ just relax ○ hug yourself ○ be grateful for this healing experience
○ something else: _____

Space for notes, words or pictures that want to express your feelings:

_____

_____

_____

_____

_____

_____

_____

Trigger Questionnaire

1. What just happened?

_____

_____

_____

2. What are you feeling right now?

○ anger ○ sadness ○ powerlessness ○ fear ○ shame ○ stress

○ despair ○ heaviness ○ emptiness ○ indefinable

○ **other feeling:** _____

3. Where is this feeling in the body?

○ neck ○ chest ○ stomach ○ arms ○ legs ○ back

○ head ○ shoulders

○ **anywhere else:** _____

4. What color is it in your mind's eye:

○ yellow ○ blue ○ red ○ green ○ black ○ gray ○ purple

○ white ○ pink ○ brown ○ colorful

○ **other color :** _____

5. What shape or form does it have:

○ distorted ○ round ball ○ constricting object ○ stone ○ water

○ fire ○ splinters ○ lightning ○ cloud ○ smoke ○ bubble ○ abyss ○ hole ○

sandstorm ○ volcanic eruption ○ fog ○ pinpricks ○ crater ○ flames

○ constricting mantle ○ **other form:** _____

. Does the feeling want to do something or act out ? If so, feel free to do
t.

○ punch a pillow ○ shake yourself ○ scream ○ draw or write something ○
pull a blanket over your head ○ yawn ○ **something else:** _____

7. **Does it want to tell you something or do words appear inside you?
What has this feeling always wanted to say and get rid of?:**

_____

_____

♡ *Take a moment and hold this side of you, understand it, talk to it, take it*

seriously ♡

8. **Do images and/or memories come up?**

○ no → continue with question 9

○ yes → go into them mentally:

**Consider the environment of the situation, relive the memory as an observer,
acknowledge the emotions at the time, intuitively change the memory
positively, e.g. with the help of an adult.**

9. **Do you feel anything different now than you did in question 2?**

○ disappointment ○ envy ○ anger ○ sadness ○ boredom

○ frustration ○ joy ○ despair ○ helplessness ○ neutral

○ other feeling: _____

*Do you find understanding for your feelings? For example, maybe you were really
just disappointed, and angry as a result? Or just angry about something that caused
you to feel powerless?*

_____

_____

10. Do you now see the situation that happened in question 1 with different eyes? How would you describe it in neutral terms?

_____

_____

_____

11. What would Love say to you now? Answer spontaneously ♡

_____

_____

_____

_____

12. If you are also open to spiritual things:
Ask inwardly for spiritual help and just be open to what comes.
You perceive: ○ loving, gentle, quiet words ○ a subtle, touching energy ○ colors that envelop and strengthen you ○ peaceful mood ○ a mental image of light-filled helpers who are simply there ○ golden light flowing into your heart ○ a basic trust in life ○ protective, invisible embrace
○ something else: _____

13. Is there anything you intuitively would like to do right now from your heart? If so, do it very much :)
○ talk to a good friend ○ go to nature ○ drink a tea ○ take a bath ○ clarify a situation from a new, clear perspective ○ be creative ○ do a hobby ○ light exercise ○ listen to music ○ just relax ○ hug yourself ○ be grateful for this healing experience
○ something else: _____

Space for notes, words or pictures that want to express your feelings:

_____

_____

_____

_____

_____

_____

_____

Trigger Questionnaire

1. What just happened?

_____

_____

_____

2. What are you feeling right now?

○ anger ○ sadness ○ powerlessness ○ fear ○ shame ○ stress

○ despair ○ heaviness ○ emptiness ○ indefinable

○ **other feeling:** _____

3. Where is this feeling in the body?

○ neck ○ chest ○ stomach ○ arms ○ legs ○ back

○ head ○ shoulders

○ **anywhere else:** _____

4. What color is it in your mind's eye:

○ yellow ○ blue ○ red ○ green ○ black ○ gray ○ purple

○ white ○ pink ○ brown ○ colorful

○ **other color :** _____

5. What shape or form does it have:

○ distorted ○ round ball ○ constricting object ○ stone ○ water

○ fire ○ splinters ○ lightning ○ cloud ○ smoke ○ bubble ○ abyss ○ hole ○

sandstorm ○ volcanic eruption ○ fog ○ pinpricks ○ crater ○ flames

○ constricting mantle ○ **other form:** _____

. Does the feeling want to do something or act out ? If so, feel free to do
t.

⊃ punch a pillow ○ shake yourself ○ scream ○ draw or write something ○
ull a blanket over your head ○ yawn ○ **something else:** _____

**7. Does it want to tell you something or do words appear inside you?
What has this feeling always wanted to say and get rid of?:**

_____

_____

♡ *Take a moment and hold this side of you, understand it, talk to it, take it*

seriously ♡

8. Do images and/or memories come up?

○ no → continue with question 9

○ yes → go into them mentally:

**Consider the environment of the situation, relive the memory as an observer,
acknowledge the emotions at the time, intuitively change the memory
positively, e.g. with the help of an adult.**

9. Do you feel anything different now than you did in question 2?

○ disappointment ○ envy ○ anger ○ sadness ○ boredom

○ frustration ○ joy ○ despair ○ helplessness ○ neutral

○ other feeling: _____

*Do you find understanding for your feelings? For example, maybe you were really
just disappointed, and angry as a result? Or just angry about something that caused
you to feel powerless?*

_____

_____

10. Do you now see the situation that happened in question 1 with different eyes? How would you describe it in neutral terms?

_____

_____

_____

11. What would Love say to you now? Answer spontaneously ♡

_____

_____

_____

_____

12. If you are also open to spiritual things:
Ask inwardly for spiritual help and just be open to what comes.

You perceive: ○ loving, gentle, quiet words ○ a subtle, touching energy ○ colors that envelop and strengthen you ○ peaceful mood ○ a mental image of light-filled helpers who are simply there ○ golden light flowing into your heart ○ a basic trust in life ○ protective, invisible embrace

○ **something else:** _____

13. Is there anything you intuitively would like to do right now from your heart? If so, do it very much :)

○ talk to a good friend ○ go to nature ○ drink a tea ○ take a bath ○ clarify a situation from a new, clear perspective ○ be creative ○ do a hobby ○ light exercise ○ listen to music ○ just relax ○ hug yourself ○ be grateful for this healing experience

○ **something else:** _____

Space for notes, words or pictures that want to express your feelings:

_____

_____

_____

_____

_____

_____

_____

Trigger Questionnaire

1. What just happened?

_____

_____

_____

2. What are you feeling right now?

○ anger ○ sadness ○ powerlessness ○ fear ○ shame ○ stress

○ despair ○ heaviness ○ emptiness ○ indefinable

○ **other feeling:** _____

3. Where is this feeling in the body?

○ neck ○ chest ○ stomach ○ arms ○ legs ○ back

○ head ○ shoulders

○ **anywhere else:** _____

4. What color is it in your mind's eye:

○ yellow ○ blue ○ red ○ green ○ black ○ gray ○ purple

○ white ○ pink ○ brown ○ colorful

○ **other color :** _____

5. What shape or form does it have:

○ distorted ○ round ball ○ constricting object ○ stone ○ water

○ fire ○ splinters ○ lightning ○ cloud ○ smoke ○ bubble ○ abyss ○ hole ○

sandstorm ○ volcanic eruption ○ fog ○ pinpricks ○ crater ○ flames

○ constricting mantle ○ **other form:** _____

. Does the feeling want to do something or act out ? If so, feel free to do
t.

⊃ punch a pillow ○ shake yourself ○ scream ○ draw or write something ○
►ull a blanket over your head ○ yawn ○ **something else:** _____

7. **Does it want to tell you something or do words appear inside you?**
What has this feeling always wanted to say and get rid of?:

_____

_____

♡ *Take a moment and hold this side of you, understand it, talk to it, take it*
seriously ♡

8. Do images and/or memories come up?

○ no → continue with question 9

○ yes → go into them mentally:
Consider the environment of the situation, relive the memory as an observer,
acknowledge the emotions at the time, intuitively change the memory
positively, e.g. with the help of an adult.

9. Do you feel anything different now than you did in question 2?

○ disappointment ○ envy ○ anger ○ sadness ○ boredom

○ frustration ○ joy ○ despair ○ helplessness ○ neutral

○ other feeling: _____

Do you find understanding for your feelings? For example, maybe you were really
just disappointed, and angry as a result? Or just angry about something that caused
you to feel powerless?

_____

_____

10. Do you now see the situation that happened in question 1 with different eyes? How would you describe it in neutral terms?

_____

_____

_____

11. What would Love say to you now? Answer spontaneously ♡

_____

_____

_____

_____

12. If you are also open to spiritual things:
Ask inwardly for spiritual help and just be open to what comes.
You perceive: ○ loving, gentle, quiet words ○ a subtle, touching energy ○ colors that envelop and strengthen you ○ peaceful mood ○ a mental image of light-filled helpers who are simply there ○ golden light flowing into your heart ○ a basic trust in life ○ protective, invisible embrace
○ **something else:** _____

13. Is there anything you intuitively would like to do right now from your heart? If so, do it very much :)
○ talk to a good friend ○ go to nature ○ drink a tea ○ take a bath ○ clarify a situation from a new, clear perspective ○ be creative ○ do a hobby ○ light exercise ○ listen to music ○ just relax ○ hug yourself ○ be grateful for this healing experience
○ **something else:** _____

Space for notes, words or pictures that want to express your feelings:

_____

_____

_____

_____

_____

_____

_____

Trigger Questionnaire

1. What just happened?

_____

_____

_____

2. What are you feeling right now?

○ anger ○ sadness ○ powerlessness ○ fear ○ shame ○ stress

○ despair ○ heaviness ○ emptiness ○ indefinable

○ **other feeling:** _____

3. Where is this feeling in the body?

○ neck ○ chest ○ stomach ○ arms ○ legs ○ back

○ head ○ shoulders

○ **anywhere else:** _____

4. What color is it in your mind's eye:

○ yellow ○ blue ○ red ○ green ○ black ○ gray ○ purple

○ white ○ pink ○ brown ○ colorful

○ **other color :** _____

5. What shape or form does it have:

○ distorted ○ round ball ○ constricting object ○ stone ○ water

○ fire ○ splinters ○ lightning ○ cloud ○ smoke ○ bubble ○ abyss ○ hole ○

sandstorm ○ volcanic eruption ○ fog ○ pinpricks ○ crater ○ flames

○ constricting mantle ○ **other form:** _____

. Does the feeling want to do something or act out ? If so, feel free to do
t.

○ punch a pillow ○ shake yourself ○ scream ○ draw or write something ○
pull a blanket over your head ○ yawn ○ **something else:** _____

7. Does it want to tell you something or do words appear inside you?
What has this feeling always wanted to say and get rid of?:

_____

_____

♡ *Take a moment and hold this side of you, understand it, talk to it, take it*

seriously ♡

8. **Do images and/or memories come up?**

○ no → continue with question 9

○ yes → go into them mentally:

Consider the environment of the situation, relive the memory as an observer,
acknowledge the emotions at the time, intuitively change the memory
positively, e.g. with the help of an adult.

9. **Do you feel anything different now than you did in question 2?**

○ disappointment ○ envy ○ anger ○ sadness ○ boredom

○ frustration ○ joy ○ despair ○ helplessness ○ neutral

○ other feeling: _____

Do you find understanding for your feelings? For example, maybe you were really
just disappointed, and angry as a result? Or just angry about something that caused
you to feel powerless?

_____

_____

10. Do you now see the situation that happened in question 1 with different eyes? How would you describe it in neutral terms?

_____

_____

_____

11. What would Love say to you now? Answer spontaneously ♡

_____

_____

_____

_____

12. If you are also open to spiritual things:
Ask inwardly for spiritual help and just be open to what comes.
You perceive: ○ loving, gentle, quiet words ○ a subtle, touching energy ○ colors that envelop and strengthen you ○ peaceful mood ○ a mental image of light-filled helpers who are simply there ○ golden light flowing into your heart ○ a basic trust in life ○ protective, invisible embrace
○ **something else:** _____

13. Is there anything you intuitively would like to do right now from your heart? If so, do it very much :)
○ talk to a good friend ○ go to nature ○ drink a tea ○ take a bath ○ clarify a situation from a new, clear perspective ○ be creative ○ do a hobby ○ light exercise ○ listen to music ○ just relax ○ hug yourself ○ be grateful for this healing experience
○ **something else:** _____

Space for notes, words or pictures that want to express your feelings:

_____

_____

_____

_____

_____

_____

_____

Trigger Questionnaire

1. What just happened?

_____

_____

_____

2. What are you feeling right now?

O anger O sadness O powerlessness O fear O shame O stress

O despair O heaviness O emptiness O indefinable

O **other feeling:** _____

3. Where is this feeling in the body?

O neck O chest O stomach O arms O legs O back

O head O shoulders

O **anywhere else:** _____

4. What color is it in your mind's eye:

O yellow O blue O red O green O black O gray O purple

O white O pink O brown O colorful

O **other color :** _____

5. What shape or form does it have:

O distorted O round ball O constricting object O stone O water

O fire O splinters O lightning O cloud O smoke O bubble O abyss O hole O

sandstorm O volcanic eruption O fog O pinpricks O crater O flames

O constricting mantle O **other form:** _____

. Does the feeling want to do something or act out ? If so, feel free to do
.

○ punch a pillow ○ shake yourself ○ scream ○ draw or write something ○
pull a blanket over your head ○ yawn ○ **something else:** _____

7. **Does it want to tell you something or do words appear inside you?**
What has this feeling always wanted to say and get rid of?:

_____

_____

♡ *Take a moment and hold this side of you, understand it, talk to it, take it*
seriously ♡

8. Do images and/or memories come up?

○ no → continue with question 9

○ yes → go into them mentally:
Consider the environment of the situation, relive the memory as an observer,
acknowledge the emotions at the time, intuitively change the memory
positively, e.g. with the help of an adult.

9. Do you feel anything different now than you did in question 2?

○ disappointment ○ envy ○ anger ○ sadness ○ boredom

○ frustration ○ joy ○ despair ○ helplessness ○ neutral

○ other feeling: _____

Do you find understanding for your feelings? For example, maybe you were really
just disappointed, and angry as a result? Or just angry about something that caused
you to feel powerless?

_____

_____

10. Do you now see the situation that happened in question 1 with different eyes? How would you describe it in neutral terms?

_____

_____

_____

11. What would Love say to you now? Answer spontaneously ♡

_____

_____

_____

_____

12. If you are also open to spiritual things:
Ask inwardly for spiritual help and just be open to what comes.

You perceive: ○ loving, gentle, quiet words ○ a subtle, touching energy ○ colors that envelop and strengthen you ○ peaceful mood ○ a mental image of light-filled helpers who are simply there ○ golden light flowing into your heart ○ a basic trust in life ○ protective, invisible embrace

○ something else: _____

13. Is there anything you intuitively would like to do right now from your heart? If so, do it very much :)

○ talk to a good friend ○ go to nature ○ drink a tea ○ take a bath ○ clarify a situation from a new, clear perspective ○ be creative ○ do a hobby ○ light exercise ○ listen to music ○ just relax ○ hug yourself ○ be grateful for this healing experience

○ something else: _____

Space for notes, words or pictures that want to express your feelings:

_____

_____

_____

_____

_____

_____

_____

_____

Trigger Questionnaire

1. What just happened?

_____

_____

_____

2. What are you feeling right now?

○ anger ○ sadness ○ powerlessness ○ fear ○ shame ○ stress

○ despair ○ heaviness ○ emptiness ○ indefinable

○ **other feeling:** _____

3. Where is this feeling in the body?

○ neck ○ chest ○ stomach ○ arms ○ legs ○ back

○ head ○ shoulders

○ **anywhere else:** _____

4. What color is it in your mind's eye:

○ yellow ○ blue ○ red ○ green ○ black ○ gray ○ purple

○ white ○ pink ○ brown ○ colorful

○ **other color :** _____

5. What shape or form does it have:

○ distorted ○ round ball ○ constricting object ○ stone ○ water

○ fire ○ splinters ○ lightning ○ cloud ○ smoke ○ bubble ○ abyss ○ hole ○

sandstorm ○ volcanic eruption ○ fog ○ pinpricks ○ crater ○ flames

○ constricting mantle ○ **other form:** _____

. Does the feeling want to do something or act out ? If so, feel free to do

:

○ punch a pillow ○ shake yourself ○ scream ○ draw or write something ○
pull a blanket over your head ○ yawn ○ **something else:** _____

7. Does it want to tell you something or do words appear inside you?
What has this feeling always wanted to say and get rid of?:

_____

_____

♡ *Take a moment and hold this side of you, understand it, talk to it, take it*
seriously ♡

8. Do images and/or memories come up?

○ no → continue with question 9

○ yes → go into them mentally:
Consider the environment of the situation, relive the memory as an observer,
acknowledge the emotions at the time, intuitively change the memory
positively, e.g. with the help of an adult.

9. Do you feel anything different now than you did in question 2?

○ disappointment ○ envy ○ anger ○ sadness ○ boredom

○ frustration ○ joy ○ despair ○ helplessness ○ neutral

○ other feeling: _____

Do you find understanding for your feelings? For example, maybe you were really
just disappointed, and angry as a result? Or just angry about something that caused
you to feel powerless?

_____

_____

10. Do you now see the situation that happened in question 1 with different eyes? How would you describe it in neutral terms?

_____

_____

_____

11. What would Love say to you now? Answer spontaneously ♡

_____

_____

_____

_____

12. If you are also open to spiritual things:
Ask inwardly for spiritual help and just be open to what comes.
You perceive: ○ loving, gentle, quiet words ○ a subtle, touching energy ○ colors that envelop and strengthen you ○ peaceful mood ○ a mental image of light-filled helpers who are simply there ○ golden light flowing into your heart ○ a basic trust in life ○ protective, invisible embrace
○ **something else:** _____

13. Is there anything you intuitively would like to do right now from your heart? If so, do it very much :)
○ talk to a good friend ○ go to nature ○ drink a tea ○ take a bath ○ clarify a situation from a new, clear perspective ○ be creative ○ do a hobby ○ light exercise ○ listen to music ○ just relax ○ hug yourself ○ be grateful for this healing experience
○ **something else:** _____

Space for notes, words or pictures that want to express your feelings:

_____

_____

_____

_____

_____

_____

_____

Trigger Questionnaire

1. What just happened?

_____

_____

_____

2. What are you feeling right now?

○ anger ○ sadness ○ powerlessness ○ fear ○ shame ○ stress

○ despair ○ heaviness ○ emptiness ○ indefinable

○ **other feeling:** _____

3. Where is this feeling in the body?

○ neck ○ chest ○ stomach ○ arms ○ legs ○ back

○ head ○ shoulders

○ **anywhere else:** _____

4. What color is it in your mind's eye:

○ yellow ○ blue ○ red ○ green ○ black ○ gray ○ purple

○ white ○ pink ○ brown ○ colorful

○ **other color :** _____

5. What shape or form does it have:

○ distorted ○ round ball ○ constricting object ○ stone ○ water

○ fire ○ splinters ○ lightning ○ cloud ○ smoke ○ bubble ○ abyss ○ hole ○

sandstorm ○ volcanic eruption ○ fog ○ pinpricks ○ crater ○ flames

○ constricting mantle ○ **other form:** _____

. Does the feeling want to do something or act out ? If so, feel free to do
.

⊃ punch a pillow ○ shake yourself ○ scream ○ draw or write something ○
ull a blanket over your head ○ yawn ○ **something else:** _____

*. Does it want to tell you something or do words appear inside you?
What has this feeling always wanted to say and get rid of?:

_____

_____

♡ *Take a moment and hold this side of you, understand it, talk to it, take it
seriously* ♡

8. Do images and/or memories come up?

○ no → continue with question 9

○ yes → go into them mentally:
Consider the environment of the situation, relive the memory as an observer,
acknowledge the emotions at the time, intuitively change the memory
positively, e.g. with the help of an adult.

9. Do you feel anything different now than you did in question 2?

○ disappointment ○ envy ○ anger ○ sadness ○ boredom

○ frustration ○ joy ○ despair ○ helplessness ○ neutral

○ other feeling: _____

*Do you find understanding for your feelings? For example, maybe you were really
just disappointed, and angry as a result? Or just angry about something that caused
you to feel powerless?*

_____

_____

10. Do you now see the situation that happened in question 1 with different eyes? How would you describe it in neutral terms?

_____

_____

_____

11. What would Love say to you now? Answer spontaneously ♡

_____

_____

_____

_____

12. If you are also open to spiritual things:
Ask inwardly for spiritual help and just be open to what comes.
You perceive: ○ loving, gentle, quiet words ○ a subtle, touching energy ○ colors that envelop and strengthen you ○ peaceful mood ○ a mental image of light-filled helpers who are simply there ○ golden light flowing into your heart ○ a basic trust in life ○ protective, invisible embrace
○ something else: _____

13. Is there anything you intuitively would like to do right now from your heart? If so, do it very much :)
○ talk to a good friend ○ go to nature ○ drink a tea ○ take a bath ○ clarify a situation from a new, clear perspective ○ be creative ○ do a hobby ○ light exercise ○ listen to music ○ just relax ○ hug yourself ○ be grateful for this healing experience
○ something else: _____

Space for notes, words or pictures that want to express your feelings:

_____

_____

_____

_____

_____

_____

_____

_____

Trigger Questionnaire

1. What just happened?

_____

_____

_____

2. What are you feeling right now?

○ anger ○ sadness ○ powerlessness ○ fear ○ shame ○ stress

○ despair ○ heaviness ○ emptiness ○ indefinable

○ **other feeling:** _____

3. Where is this feeling in the body?

○ neck ○ chest ○ stomach ○ arms ○ legs ○ back

○ head ○ shoulders

○ **anywhere else:** _____

4. What color is it in your mind's eye:

○ yellow ○ blue ○ red ○ green ○ black ○ gray ○ purple

○ white ○ pink ○ brown ○ colorful

○ **other color :** _____

5. What shape or form does it have:

○ distorted ○ round ball ○ constricting object ○ stone ○ water

○ fire ○ splinters ○ lightning ○ cloud ○ smoke ○ bubble ○ abyss ○ hole ○

sandstorm ○ volcanic eruption ○ fog ○ pinpricks ○ crater ○ flames

○ constricting mantle ○ **other form:** _____

. Does the feeling want to do something or act out ? If so, feel free to do

.

◦ punch a pillow ◦ shake yourself ◦ scream ◦ draw or write something ◦
◦ull a blanket over your head ◦ yawn ◦ **something else:** _____

. Does it want to tell you something or do words appear inside you?
What has this feeling always wanted to say and get rid of?:

_____

_____

♡ *Take a moment and hold this side of you, understand it, talk to it, take it*
seriously ♡

8. Do images and/or memories come up?
◦ no → continue with question 9
◦ yes → go into them mentally:
Consider the environment of the situation, relive the memory as an observer,
acknowledge the emotions at the time, intuitively change the memory
positively, e.g. with the help of an adult.

9. Do you feel anything different now than you did in question 2?
◦ disappointment ◦ envy ◦ anger ◦ sadness ◦ boredom
◦ frustration ◦ joy ◦ despair ◦ helplessness ◦ neutral
◦ other feeling: _____
Do you find understanding for your feelings? For example, maybe you were really
just disappointed, and angry as a result? Or just angry about something that caused
you to feel powerless?

_____

_____

10. Do you now see the situation that happened in question 1 with different eyes? How would you describe it in neutral terms?

_____

_____

_____

11. What would Love say to you now? Answer spontaneously ♡

_____

_____

_____

_____

12. If you are also open to spiritual things:
Ask inwardly for spiritual help and just be open to what comes.
You perceive: ○ loving, gentle, quiet words ○ a subtle, touching energy ○ colors that envelop and strengthen you ○ peaceful mood ○ a mental image of light-filled helpers who are simply there ○ golden light flowing into your heart ○ a basic trust in life ○ protective, invisible embrace
○ something else: _____

13. Is there anything you intuitively would like to do right now from your heart? If so, do it very much :)
○ talk to a good friend ○ go to nature ○ drink a tea ○ take a bath ○ clarify a situation from a new, clear perspective ○ be creative ○ do a hobby ○ light exercise ○ listen to music ○ just relax ○ hug yourself ○ be grateful for this healing experience
○ something else: _____

Space for notes, words or pictures that want to express your feelings:

_____

_____

_____

_____

_____

_____

_____

_____

Trigger Questionnaire

1. What just happened?

_____

_____

_____

2. What are you feeling right now?

○ anger ○ sadness ○ powerlessness ○ fear ○ shame ○ stress

○ despair ○ heaviness ○ emptiness ○ indefinable

○ **other feeling:** _____

3. Where is this feeling in the body?

○ neck ○ chest ○ stomach ○ arms ○ legs ○ back

○ head ○ shoulders

○ **anywhere else:** _____

4. What color is it in your mind's eye:

○ yellow ○ blue ○ red ○ green ○ black ○ gray ○ purple

○ white ○ pink ○ brown ○ colorful

○ **other color :** _____

5. What shape or form does it have:

○ distorted ○ round ball ○ constricting object ○ stone ○ water

○ fire ○ splinters ○ lightning ○ cloud ○ smoke ○ bubble ○ abyss ○ hole ○

sandstorm ○ volcanic eruption ○ fog ○ pinpricks ○ crater ○ flames

○ constricting mantle ○ **other form:** _____

. Does the feeling want to do something or act out ? If so, feel free to do

.

› punch a pillow ○ shake yourself ○ scream ○ draw or write something ○ ull a blanket over your head ○ yawn ○ **something else:** _____

'. Does it want to tell you something or do words appear inside you? Vhat has this feeling always wanted to say and get rid of?:

_____

_____

♡ *Take a moment and hold this side of you, understand it, talk to it, take it* *seriously* ♡

8. Do images and/or memories come up?

○ no → continue with question 9

○ yes → go into them mentally:

Consider the environment of the situation, relive the memory as an observer, acknowledge the emotions at the time, intuitively change the memory positively, e.g. with the help of an adult.

9. Do you feel anything different now than you did in question 2?

○ disappointment ○ envy ○ anger ○ sadness ○ boredom

○ frustration ○ joy ○ despair ○ helplessness ○ neutral

○ other feeling: _____

Do you find understanding for your feelings? For example, maybe you were really *just disappointed, and angry as a result? Or just angry about something that caused* *you to feel powerless?*

_____

_____

10. Do you now see the situation that happened in question 1 with different eyes? How would you describe it in neutral terms?

_____

_____

_____

11. What would Love say to you now? Answer spontaneously ♡

_____

_____

_____

_____

12. If you are also open to spiritual things:
Ask inwardly for spiritual help and just be open to what comes.
You perceive: ○ loving, gentle, quiet words ○ a subtle, touching energy ○ colors that envelop and strengthen you ○ peaceful mood ○ a mental image of light-filled helpers who are simply there ○ golden light flowing into your heart ○ a basic trust in life ○ protective, invisible embrace
○ **something else:** _____

13. Is there anything you intuitively would like to do right now from your heart? If so, do it very much :)
○ talk to a good friend ○ go to nature ○ drink a tea ○ take a bath ○ clarify a situation from a new, clear perspective ○ be creative ○ do a hobby ○ light exercise ○ listen to music ○ just relax ○ hug yourself ○ be grateful for this healing experience
○ **something else:** _____

Space for notes, words or pictures that want to express your feelings:

_____

_____

_____

_____

_____

_____

_____

_____

Trigger Questionnaire

1. What just happened?

_____

_____

_____

2. What are you feeling right now?

○ anger ○ sadness ○ powerlessness ○ fear ○ shame ○ stress

○ despair ○ heaviness ○ emptiness ○ indefinable

○ **other feeling:** _____

3. Where is this feeling in the body?

○ neck ○ chest ○ stomach ○ arms ○ legs ○ back

○ head ○ shoulders

○ **anywhere else:** _____

4. What color is it in your mind's eye:

○ yellow ○ blue ○ red ○ green ○ black ○ gray ○ purple

○ white ○ pink ○ brown ○ colorful

○ **other color :** _____

5. What shape or form does it have:

○ distorted ○ round ball ○ constricting object ○ stone ○ water

○ fire ○ splinters ○ lightning ○ cloud ○ smoke ○ bubble ○ abyss ○ hole ○

sandstorm ○ volcanic eruption ○ fog ○ pinpricks ○ crater ○ flames

○ constricting mantle ○ **other form:** _____

. Does the feeling want to do something or act out ? If so, feel free to do

.

 punch a pillow ○ shake yourself ○ scream ○ draw or write something ○

 ull a blanket over your head ○ yawn ○ **something else:** _____

. Does it want to tell you something or do words appear inside you?
What has this feeling always wanted to say and get rid of?:

_____

_____

♡ *Take a moment and hold this side of you, understand it, talk to it, take it*
seriously ♡

8. **Do images and/or memories come up?**

○ no → continue with question 9

○ yes → go into them mentally:
Consider the environment of the situation, relive the memory as an observer,
acknowledge the emotions at the time, intuitively change the memory
positively, e.g. with the help of an adult.

9. **Do you feel anything different now than you did in question 2?**

○ disappointment ○ envy ○ anger ○ sadness ○ boredom

○ frustration ○ joy ○ despair ○ helplessness ○ neutral

○ other feeling: _____

Do you find understanding for your feelings? For example, maybe you were really
just disappointed, and angry as a result? Or just angry about something that caused
you to feel powerless?

_____

_____

10. Do you now see the situation that happened in question 1 with different eyes? How would you describe it in neutral terms?

_____

_____

_____

11. What would Love say to you now? Answer spontaneously ♡

_____

_____

_____

_____

12. If you are also open to spiritual things:
Ask inwardly for spiritual help and just be open to what comes.

You perceive: ○ loving, gentle, quiet words ○ a subtle, touching energy ○ colors that envelop and strengthen you ○ peaceful mood ○ a mental image of light-filled helpers who are simply there ○ golden light flowing into your heart ○ a basic trust in life ○ protective, invisible embrace

○ something else: _____

13. Is there anything you intuitively would like to do right now from your heart? If so, do it very much :)

○ talk to a good friend ○ go to nature ○ drink a tea ○ take a bath ○ clarify a situation from a new, clear perspective ○ be creative ○ do a hobby ○ light exercise ○ listen to music ○ just relax ○ hug yourself ○ be grateful for this healing experience

○ something else: _____

Space for notes, words or pictures that want to express your feelings:

_____

_____

_____

_____

_____

_____

_____

_____

Trigger Questionnaire

1. What just happened?

_____
_____
_____

2. What are you feeling right now?

○ anger ○ sadness ○ powerlessness ○ fear ○ shame ○ stress

○ despair ○ heaviness ○ emptiness ○ indefinable

○ **other feeling:** _____

3. Where is this feeling in the body?

○ neck ○ chest ○ stomach ○ arms ○ legs ○ back

○ head ○ shoulders

○ **anywhere else:** _____

4. What color is it in your mind's eye:

○ yellow ○ blue ○ red ○ green ○ black ○ gray ○ purple

○ white ○ pink ○ brown ○ colorful

○ **other color :** _____

5. What shape or form does it have:

○ distorted ○ round ball ○ constricting object ○ stone ○ water

○ fire ○ splinters ○ lightning ○ cloud ○ smoke ○ bubble ○ abyss ○ hole ○

sandstorm ○ volcanic eruption ○ fog ○ pinpricks ○ crater ○ flames

○ constricting mantle ○ **other form:** _____

. Does the feeling want to do something or act out ? If so, feel free to do
.

◦ punch a pillow ○ shake yourself ○ scream ○ draw or write something ○
ull a blanket over your head ○ yawn ○ **something else:** _____

. Does it want to tell you something or do words appear inside you?
What has this feeling always wanted to say and get rid of?:

_____

_____

♡ *Take a moment and hold this side of you, understand it, talk to it, take it*
seriously ♡

8. Do images and/or memories come up?
○ no → continue with question 9
○ yes → go into them mentally:
Consider the environment of the situation, relive the memory as an observer,
acknowledge the emotions at the time, intuitively change the memory
positively, e.g. with the help of an adult.

9. Do you feel anything different now than you did in question 2?
○ disappointment ○ envy ○ anger ○ sadness ○ boredom
○ frustration ○ joy ○ despair ○ helplessness ○ neutral
○ other feeling: _____
Do you find understanding for your feelings? For example, maybe you were really
just disappointed, and angry as a result? Or just angry about something that caused
you to feel powerless?

_____

_____

10. Do you now see the situation that happened in question 1 with different eyes? How would you describe it in neutral terms?

_____

_____

_____

11. What would Love say to you now? Answer spontaneously ♡

_____

_____

_____

_____

12. If you are also open to spiritual things:
Ask inwardly for spiritual help and just be open to what comes.

You perceive: ○ loving, gentle, quiet words ○ a subtle, touching energy ○ colors that envelop and strengthen you ○ peaceful mood ○ a mental image of light-filled helpers who are simply there ○ golden light flowing into your heart ○ a basic trust in life ○ protective, invisible embrace

○ something else: _____

13. Is there anything you intuitively would like to do right now from your heart? If so, do it very much :)

○ talk to a good friend ○ go to nature ○ drink a tea ○ take a bath ○ clarify a situation from a new, clear perspective ○ be creative ○ do a hobby ○ light exercise ○ listen to music ○ just relax ○ hug yourself ○ be grateful for this healing experience

○ something else: _____

Space for notes, words or pictures that want to express your feelings:

_____

_____

_____

_____

_____

_____

_____

Trigger Questionnaire

1. What just happened?

_____

_____

_____

2. What are you feeling right now?

○ anger ○ sadness ○ powerlessness ○ fear ○ shame ○ stress

○ despair ○ heaviness ○ emptiness ○ indefinable

○ **other feeling:** _____

3. Where is this feeling in the body?

○ neck ○ chest ○ stomach ○ arms ○ legs ○ back

○ head ○ shoulders

○ **anywhere else:** _____

4. What color is it in your mind's eye:

○ yellow ○ blue ○ red ○ green ○ black ○ gray ○ purple

○ white ○ pink ○ brown ○ colorful

○ **other color :** _____

5. What shape or form does it have:

○ distorted ○ round ball ○ constricting object ○ stone ○ water

○ fire ○ splinters ○ lightning ○ cloud ○ smoke ○ bubble ○ abyss ○ hole ○

sandstorm ○ volcanic eruption ○ fog ○ pinpricks ○ crater ○ flames

○ constricting mantle ○ **other form:** _____

. Does the feeling want to do something or act out ? If so, feel free to do
.

punch a pillow ○ shake yourself ○ scream ○ draw or write something ○
ull a blanket over your head ○ yawn ○ **something else:** _____

. Does it want to tell you something or do words appear inside you?
Vhat has this feeling always wanted to say and get rid of?:

_____

_____

♡ *Take a moment and hold this side of you, understand it, talk to it, take it*
eriously ♡

3. **Do images and/or memories come up?**

○ no → continue with question 9

○ yes → go into them mentally:
Consider the environment of the situation, relive the memory as an observer,
acknowledge the emotions at the time, intuitively change the memory
positively, e.g. with the help of an adult.

9. **Do you feel anything different now than you did in question 2?**

○ disappointment ○ envy ○ anger ○ sadness ○ boredom

○ frustration ○ joy ○ despair ○ helplessness ○ neutral

○ other feeling: _____

Do you find understanding for your feelings? For example, maybe you were really
just disappointed, and angry as a result? Or just angry about something that caused
you to feel powerless?

_____

_____

10. Do you now see the situation that happened in question 1 with different eyes? How would you describe it in neutral terms?

_____

_____

_____

11. What would Love say to you now? Answer spontaneously ♡

_____

_____

_____

_____

12. If you are also open to spiritual things:
Ask inwardly for spiritual help and just be open to what comes.
You perceive: ○ loving, gentle, quiet words ○ a subtle, touching energy ○ colors that envelop and strengthen you ○ peaceful mood ○ a mental image of light-filled helpers who are simply there ○ golden light flowing into your heart ○ a basic trust in life ○ protective, invisible embrace
○ **something else:** _____

13. Is there anything you intuitively would like to do right now from your heart? If so, do it very much :)
○ talk to a good friend ○ go to nature ○ drink a tea ○ take a bath ○ clarify a situation from a new, clear perspective ○ be creative ○ do a hobby ○ light exercise ○ listen to music ○ just relax ○ hug yourself ○ be grateful for this healing experience
○ **something else:** _____

Space for notes, words or pictures that want to express your feelings:

_____

_____

_____

_____

_____

_____

_____

_____

Trigger Questionnaire

1. What just happened?

_____

_____

_____

2. What are you feeling right now?

○ anger ○ sadness ○ powerlessness ○ fear ○ shame ○ stress

○ despair ○ heaviness ○ emptiness ○ indefinable

○ **other feeling:** _____

3. Where is this feeling in the body?

○ neck ○ chest ○ stomach ○ arms ○ legs ○ back

○ head ○ shoulders

○ **anywhere else:** _____

4. What color is it in your mind's eye:

○ yellow ○ blue ○ red ○ green ○ black ○ gray ○ purple

○ white ○ pink ○ brown ○ colorful

○ **other color :** _____

5. What shape or form does it have:

○ distorted ○ round ball ○ constricting object ○ stone ○ water

○ fire ○ splinters ○ lightning ○ cloud ○ smoke ○ bubble ○ abyss ○ hole ○

sandstorm ○ volcanic eruption ○ fog ○ pinpricks ○ crater ○ flames

○ constricting mantle ○ **other form:** _____

. Does the feeling want to do something or act out ? If so, feel free to do

punch a pillow ○ shake yourself ○ scream ○ draw or write something ○
ull a blanket over your head ○ yawn ○ **something else:** _____

. Does it want to tell you something or do words appear inside you?
What has this feeling always wanted to say and get rid of?:

_____

_____

♡ *Take a moment and hold this side of you, understand it, talk to it, take it*
seriously ♡

8. Do images and/or memories come up?
○ no → continue with question 9
○ yes → go into them mentally:
Consider the environment of the situation, relive the memory as an observer,
acknowledge the emotions at the time, intuitively change the memory
positively, e.g. with the help of an adult.

9. Do you feel anything different now than you did in question 2?
○ disappointment ○ envy ○ anger ○ sadness ○ boredom
○ frustration ○ joy ○ despair ○ helplessness ○ neutral
○ other feeling: _____
Do you find understanding for your feelings? For example, maybe you were really
just disappointed, and angry as a result? Or just angry about something that caused
you to feel powerless?

_____

_____

10. Do you now see the situation that happened in question 1 with different eyes? How would you describe it in neutral terms?

_____

_____

_____

11. What would Love say to you now? Answer spontaneously ♡

_____

_____

_____

_____

12. If you are also open to spiritual things:
Ask inwardly for spiritual help and just be open to what comes.
You perceive: ○ loving, gentle, quiet words ○ a subtle, touching energy ○ colors that envelop and strengthen you ○ peaceful mood ○ a mental image of light-filled helpers who are simply there ○ golden light flowing into your heart ○ a basic trust in life ○ protective, invisible embrace
○ **something else:** _____

13. Is there anything you intuitively would like to do right now from your heart? If so, do it very much :)
○ talk to a good friend ○ go to nature ○ drink a tea ○ take a bath ○ clarify a situation from a new, clear perspective ○ be creative ○ do a hobby ○ light exercise ○ listen to music ○ just relax ○ hug yourself ○ be grateful for this healing experience
○ **something else:** _____

Space for notes, words or pictures that want to express your feelings:

_____

_____

_____

_____

_____

_____

_____

Trigger Questionnaire

1. What just happened?

_____

_____

_____

2. What are you feeling right now?

○ anger ○ sadness ○ powerlessness ○ fear ○ shame ○ stress

○ despair ○ heaviness ○ emptiness ○ indefinable

○ **other feeling:** _____

3. Where is this feeling in the body?

○ neck ○ chest ○ stomach ○ arms ○ legs ○ back

○ head ○ shoulders

○ **anywhere else:** _____

4. What color is it in your mind's eye:

○ yellow ○ blue ○ red ○ green ○ black ○ gray ○ purple

○ white ○ pink ○ brown ○ colorful

○ **other color :** _____

5. What shape or form does it have:

○ distorted ○ round ball ○ constricting object ○ stone ○ water

○ fire ○ splinters ○ lightning ○ cloud ○ smoke ○ bubble ○ abyss ○ hole ○

sandstorm ○ volcanic eruption ○ fog ○ pinpricks ○ crater ○ flames

○ constricting mantle ○ **other form:** _____

. Does the feeling want to do something or act out ? If so, feel free to do
.

○ punch a pillow ○ shake yourself ○ scream ○ draw or write something ○
○ull a blanket over your head ○ yawn ○ **something else:** _____

. Does it want to tell you something or do words appear inside you?
What has this feeling always wanted to say and get rid of?:

_____

_____

♡ *Take a moment and hold this side of you, understand it, talk to it, take it*
seriously ♡

8. Do images and/or memories come up?

○ no → continue with question 9

○ yes → go into them mentally:

Consider the environment of the situation, relive the memory as an observer,
acknowledge the emotions at the time, intuitively change the memory
positively, e.g. with the help of an adult.

9. Do you feel anything different now than you did in question 2?

○ disappointment ○ envy ○ anger ○ sadness ○ boredom

○ frustration ○ joy ○ despair ○ helplessness ○ neutral

○ other feeling: _____

Do you find understanding for your feelings? For example, maybe you were really
just disappointed, and angry as a result? Or just angry about something that caused
you to feel powerless?

_____

_____

10. Do you now see the situation that happened in question 1 with different eyes? How would you describe it in neutral terms?

_____

_____

_____

11. What would Love say to you now? Answer spontaneously ♡

_____

_____

_____

_____

12. If you are also open to spiritual things:

Ask inwardly for spiritual help and just be open to what comes.

You perceive: ○ loving, gentle, quiet words ○ a subtle, touching energy ○ colors that envelop and strengthen you ○ peaceful mood ○ a mental image of light-filled helpers who are simply there ○ golden light flowing into your heart ○ a basic trust in life ○ protective, invisible embrace

○ **something else:** _____

13. Is there anything you intuitively would like to do right now from your heart? If so, do it very much :)

○ talk to a good friend ○ go to nature ○ drink a tea ○ take a bath ○ clarify a situation from a new, clear perspective ○ be creative ○ do a hobby ○ light exercise ○ listen to music ○ just relax ○ hug yourself ○ be grateful for this healing experience

○ **something else:** _____

Space for notes, words or pictures that want to express your feelings:

_____

_____

_____

_____

_____

_____

_____

Trigger Questionnaire

1. What just happened?

_____

_____

_____

2. What are you feeling right now?

○ anger ○ sadness ○ powerlessness ○ fear ○ shame ○ stress

○ despair ○ heaviness ○ emptiness ○ indefinable

○ **other feeling:** _____

3. Where is this feeling in the body?

○ neck ○ chest ○ stomach ○ arms ○ legs ○ back

○ head ○ shoulders

○ **anywhere else:** _____

4. What color is it in your mind's eye:

○ yellow ○ blue ○ red ○ green ○ black ○ gray ○ purple

○ white ○ pink ○ brown ○ colorful

○ **other color :** _____

5. What shape or form does it have:

○ distorted ○ round ball ○ constricting object ○ stone ○ water

○ fire ○ splinters ○ lightning ○ cloud ○ smoke ○ bubble ○ abyss ○ hole ○

sandstorm ○ volcanic eruption ○ fog ○ pinpricks ○ crater ○ flames

○ constricting mantle ○ **other form:** _____

. Does the feeling want to do something or act out ? If so, feel free to do

.

punch a pillow ○ shake yourself ○ scream ○ draw or write something ○
pull a blanket over your head ○ yawn ○ **something else:** _____

. Does it want to tell you something or do words appear inside you?
What has this feeling always wanted to say and get rid of?:

_____

_____

♡ *Take a moment and hold this side of you, understand it, talk to it, take it
seriously* ♡

8. Do images and/or memories come up?

○ no → continue with question 9

○ yes → go into them mentally:
Consider the environment of the situation, relive the memory as an observer,
acknowledge the emotions at the time, intuitively change the memory
positively, e.g. with the help of an adult.

9. Do you feel anything different now than you did in question 2?

○ disappointment ○ envy ○ anger ○ sadness ○ boredom
○ frustration ○ joy ○ despair ○ helplessness ○ neutral
○ other feeling: _____
*Do you find understanding for your feelings? For example, maybe you were really
just disappointed, and angry as a result? Or just angry about something that caused
you to feel powerless?*

_____

_____

10. Do you now see the situation that happened in question 1 with different eyes? How would you describe it in neutral terms?

_____

_____

_____

11. What would Love say to you now? Answer spontaneously ♡

_____

_____

_____

_____

12. If you are also open to spiritual things:

Ask inwardly for spiritual help and just be open to what comes.

You perceive: ○ loving, gentle, quiet words ○ a subtle, touching energy ○ colors that envelop and strengthen you ○ peaceful mood ○ a mental image of light-filled helpers who are simply there ○ golden light flowing into your heart ○ a basic trust in life ○ protective, invisible embrace

○ **something else:** _____

13. Is there anything you intuitively would like to do right now from your heart? If so, do it very much :)

○ talk to a good friend ○ go to nature ○ drink a tea ○ take a bath ○ clarify a situation from a new, clear perspective ○ be creative ○ do a hobby ○ light exercise ○ listen to music ○ just relax ○ hug yourself ○ be grateful for this healing experience

○ **something else:** _____

Space for notes, words or pictures that want to express your feelings:

_____

_____

_____

_____

_____

_____

_____

_____

Trigger Questionnaire

1. What just happened?

_____

_____

_____

2. What are you feeling right now?

○ anger ○ sadness ○ powerlessness ○ fear ○ shame ○ stress

○ despair ○ heaviness ○ emptiness ○ indefinable

○ **other feeling:** _____

3. Where is this feeling in the body?

○ neck ○ chest ○ stomach ○ arms ○ legs ○ back

○ head ○ shoulders

○ **anywhere else:** _____

4. What color is it in your mind's eye:

○ yellow ○ blue ○ red ○ green ○ black ○ gray ○ purple

○ white ○ pink ○ brown ○ colorful

○ **other color :** _____

5. What shape or form does it have:

○ distorted ○ round ball ○ constricting object ○ stone ○ water

○ fire ○ splinters ○ lightning ○ cloud ○ smoke ○ bubble ○ abyss ○ hole ○

sandstorm ○ volcanic eruption ○ fog ○ pinpricks ○ crater ○ flames

○ constricting mantle ○ **other form:** _____

. Does the feeling want to do something or act out ? If so, feel free to do

punch a pillow ○ shake yourself ○ scream ○ draw or write something ○
pull a blanket over your head ○ yawn ○ **something else:** _____

. Does it want to tell you something or do words appear inside you?
What has this feeling always wanted to say and get rid of?:
_____
_____

♡ *Take a moment and hold this side of you, understand it, talk to it, take it*
seriously ♡

8. **Do images and/or memories come up?**
○ no → continue with question 9
○ yes → go into them mentally:
Consider the environment of the situation, relive the memory as an observer,
acknowledge the emotions at the time, intuitively change the memory
positively, e.g. with the help of an adult.

9. **Do you feel anything different now than you did in question 2?**
○ disappointment ○ envy ○ anger ○ sadness ○ boredom
○ frustration ○ joy ○ despair ○ helplessness ○ neutral
○ other feeling: _____
Do you find understanding for your feelings? For example, maybe you were really
just disappointed, and angry as a result? Or just angry about something that caused
you to feel powerless?
_____
_____

10. Do you now see the situation that happened in question 1 with different eyes? How would you describe it in neutral terms?

_____

_____

_____

11. What would Love say to you now? Answer spontaneously ♡

_____

_____

_____

_____

12. If you are also open to spiritual things:
Ask inwardly for spiritual help and just be open to what comes.
You perceive: ○ loving, gentle, quiet words ○ a subtle, touching energy ○ colors that envelop and strengthen you ○ peaceful mood ○ a mental image of light-filled helpers who are simply there ○ golden light flowing into your heart ○ a basic trust in life ○ protective, invisible embrace
○ something else: _____

13. Is there anything you intuitively would like to do right now from your heart? If so, do it very much :)
○ talk to a good friend ○ go to nature ○ drink a tea ○ take a bath ○ clarify a situation from a new, clear perspective ○ be creative ○ do a hobby ○ light exercise ○ listen to music ○ just relax ○ hug yourself ○ be grateful for this healing experience
○ **something else:** _____

Space for notes, words or pictures that want to express your feelings:

_____

_____

_____

_____

_____

_____

_____

_____

Trigger Questionnaire

1. What just happened?

_____

_____

_____

2. What are you feeling right now?

○ anger ○ sadness ○ powerlessness ○ fear ○ shame ○ stress

○ despair ○ heaviness ○ emptiness ○ indefinable

○ **other feeling:** _____

3. Where is this feeling in the body?

○ neck ○ chest ○ stomach ○ arms ○ legs ○ back

○ head ○ shoulders

○ **anywhere else:** _____

4. What color is it in your mind's eye:

○ yellow ○ blue ○ red ○ green ○ black ○ gray ○ purple

○ white ○ pink ○ brown ○ colorful

○ **other color :** _____

5. What shape or form does it have:

○ distorted ○ round ball ○ constricting object ○ stone ○ water

○ fire ○ splinters ○ lightning ○ cloud ○ smoke ○ bubble ○ abyss ○ hole ○

sandstorm ○ volcanic eruption ○ fog ○ pinpricks ○ crater ○ flames

○ constricting mantle ○ **other form:** _____

. Does the feeling want to do something or act out ? If so, feel free to do

punch a pillow ○ shake yourself ○ scream ○ draw or write something ○ ull a blanket over your head ○ yawn ○ **something else:** _____

. Does it want to tell you something or do words appear inside you? Vhat has this feeling always wanted to say and get rid of?:

_____

_____

♡ *Take a moment and hold this side of you, understand it, talk to it, take it eriously* ♡

. **Do images and/or memories come up?**

○ no → continue with question 9

○ yes → go into them mentally:

Consider the environment of the situation, relive the memory as an observer, acknowledge the emotions at the time, intuitively change the memory positively, e.g. with the help of an adult.

9. **Do you feel anything different now than you did in question 2?**

○ disappointment ○ envy ○ anger ○ sadness ○ boredom

○ frustration ○ joy ○ despair ○ helplessness ○ neutral

○ other feeling: _____

Do you find understanding for your feelings? For example, maybe you were really just disappointed, and angry as a result? Or just angry about something that caused you to feel powerless?

_____

_____

10. Do you now see the situation that happened in question 1 with different eyes? How would you describe it in neutral terms?

_____

_____

_____

11. What would Love say to you now? Answer spontaneously ♡

_____

_____

_____

_____

12. If you are also open to spiritual things:
Ask inwardly for spiritual help and just be open to what comes.

You perceive: ○ loving, gentle, quiet words ○ a subtle, touching energy ○ colors that envelop and strengthen you ○ peaceful mood ○ a mental image of light-filled helpers who are simply there ○ golden light flowing into your heart ○ a basic trust in life ○ protective, invisible embrace

○ something else: _____

13. Is there anything you intuitively would like to do right now from your heart? If so, do it very much :)

○ talk to a good friend ○ go to nature ○ drink a tea ○ take a bath ○ clarify a situation from a new, clear perspective ○ be creative ○ do a hobby ○ light exercise ○ listen to music ○ just relax ○ hug yourself ○ be grateful for this healing experience

○ something else: _____

Space for notes, words or pictures that want to express your feelings:

_____

_____

_____

_____

_____

_____

_____

Trigger Questionnaire

1. What just happened?

_____

_____

_____

2. What are you feeling right now?

○ anger ○ sadness ○ powerlessness ○ fear ○ shame ○ stress

○ despair ○ heaviness ○ emptiness ○ indefinable

○ **other feeling:** _____

3. Where is this feeling in the body?

○ neck ○ chest ○ stomach ○ arms ○ legs ○ back

○ head ○ shoulders

○ **anywhere else:** _____

4. What color is it in your mind's eye:

○ yellow ○ blue ○ red ○ green ○ black ○ gray ○ purple

○ white ○ pink ○ brown ○ colorful

○ **other color :** _____

5. What shape or form does it have:

○ distorted ○ round ball ○ constricting object ○ stone ○ water

○ fire ○ splinters ○ lightning ○ cloud ○ smoke ○ bubble ○ abyss ○ hole ○

sandstorm ○ volcanic eruption ○ fog ○ pinpricks ○ crater ○ flames

○ constricting mantle ○ **other form:** _____

. Does the feeling want to do something or act out ? If so, feel free to do
.

punch a pillow ○ shake yourself ○ scream ○ draw or write something ○
pull a blanket over your head ○ yawn ○ **something else:** _____

. Does it want to tell you something or do words appear inside you?
What has this feeling always wanted to say and get rid of?:

_____

_____

*♡ Take a moment and hold this side of you, understand it, talk to it, take it
seriously ♡*

8. Do images and/or memories come up?

○ no → continue with question 9
○ yes → go into them mentally:
Consider the environment of the situation, relive the memory as an observer,
acknowledge the emotions at the time, intuitively change the memory
positively, e.g. with the help of an adult.

9. Do you feel anything different now than you did in question 2?

○ disappointment ○ envy ○ anger ○ sadness ○ boredom
○ frustration ○ joy ○ despair ○ helplessness ○ neutral
○ other feeling: _____

*Do you find understanding for your feelings? For example, maybe you were really
just disappointed, and angry as a result? Or just angry about something that caused
you to feel powerless?*

_____

_____

10. Do you now see the situation that happened in question 1 with different eyes? How would you describe it in neutral terms?

_____

_____

_____

11. What would Love say to you now? Answer spontaneously ♡

_____

_____

_____

_____

12. If you are also open to spiritual things:
Ask inwardly for spiritual help and just be open to what comes.
You perceive: ○ loving, gentle, quiet words ○ a subtle, touching energy ○ colors that envelop and strengthen you ○ peaceful mood ○ a mental image of light-filled helpers who are simply there ○ golden light flowing into your heart ○ a basic trust in life ○ protective, invisible embrace
○ **something else:** _____

13. Is there anything you intuitively would like to do right now from your heart? If so, do it very much :)
○ talk to a good friend ○ go to nature ○ drink a tea ○ take a bath ○ clarify a situation from a new, clear perspective ○ be creative ○ do a hobby ○ light exercise ○ listen to music ○ just relax ○ hug yourself ○ be grateful for this healing experience
○ **something else:** _____

Space for notes, words or pictures that want to express your feelings:

_____

_____

_____

_____

_____

_____

_____

Trigger Questionnaire

1. What just happened?

_____

_____

_____

2. What are you feeling right now?

○ anger ○ sadness ○ powerlessness ○ fear ○ shame ○ stress

○ despair ○ heaviness ○ emptiness ○ indefinable

○ **other feeling:** _____

3. Where is this feeling in the body?

○ neck ○ chest ○ stomach ○ arms ○ legs ○ back

○ head ○ shoulders

○ **anywhere else:** _____

4. What color is it in your mind's eye:

○ yellow ○ blue ○ red ○ green ○ black ○ gray ○ purple

○ white ○ pink ○ brown ○ colorful

○ **other color :** _____

5. What shape or form does it have:

○ distorted ○ round ball ○ constricting object ○ stone ○ water

○ fire ○ splinters ○ lightning ○ cloud ○ smoke ○ bubble ○ abyss ○ hole ○ sandstorm ○ volcanic eruption ○ fog ○ pinpricks ○ crater ○ flames

○ constricting mantle ○ **other form:** _____

. Does the feeling want to do something or act out ? If so, feel free to do

· punch a pillow ○ shake yourself ○ scream ○ draw or write something ○
ull a blanket over your head ○ yawn ○ **something else:** _____

. Does it want to tell you something or do words appear inside you?
What has this feeling always wanted to say and get rid of?:

_____

_____

♡ *Take a moment and hold this side of you, understand it, talk to it, take it*
seriously ♡

3. Do images and/or memories come up?
○ no → continue with question 9
○ yes → go into them mentally:
Consider the environment of the situation, relive the memory as an observer,
acknowledge the emotions at the time, intuitively change the memory
positively, e.g. with the help of an adult.

9. Do you feel anything different now than you did in question 2?
○ disappointment ○ envy ○ anger ○ sadness ○ boredom
○ frustration ○ joy ○ despair ○ helplessness ○ neutral
○ other feeling: _____
Do you find understanding for your feelings? For example, maybe you were really
just disappointed, and angry as a result? Or just angry about something that caused
you to feel powerless?

_____

_____

10. Do you now see the situation that happened in question 1 with different eyes? How would you describe it in neutral terms?

_____

_____

_____

11. What would Love say to you now? Answer spontaneously ♡

_____

_____

_____

_____

12. If you are also open to spiritual things:
Ask inwardly for spiritual help and just be open to what comes.
You perceive: ○ loving, gentle, quiet words ○ a subtle, touching energy ○ colors that envelop and strengthen you ○ peaceful mood ○ a mental image of light-filled helpers who are simply there ○ golden light flowing into your heart ○ a basic trust in life ○ protective, invisible embrace
○ **something else:** _____

13. Is there anything you intuitively would like to do right now from your heart? If so, do it very much :)
○ talk to a good friend ○ go to nature ○ drink a tea ○ take a bath ○ clarify a situation from a new, clear perspective ○ be creative ○ do a hobby ○ light exercise ○ listen to music ○ just relax ○ hug yourself ○ be grateful for this healing experience
○ **something else:** _____

Space for notes, words or pictures that want to express your feelings:

_____

_____

_____

_____

_____

_____

_____

_____

Trigger Questionnaire

1. What just happened?

_____

_____

_____

2. What are you feeling right now?

○ anger ○ sadness ○ powerlessness ○ fear ○ shame ○ stress

○ despair ○ heaviness ○ emptiness ○ indefinable

○ **other feeling:** _____

3. Where is this feeling in the body?

○ neck ○ chest ○ stomach ○ arms ○ legs ○ back

○ head ○ shoulders

○ **anywhere else:** _____

4. What color is it in your mind's eye:

○ yellow ○ blue ○ red ○ green ○ black ○ gray ○ purple

○ white ○ pink ○ brown ○ colorful

○ **other color :** _____

5. What shape or form does it have:

○ distorted ○ round ball ○ constricting object ○ stone ○ water

○ fire ○ splinters ○ lightning ○ cloud ○ smoke ○ bubble ○ abyss ○ hole ○

sandstorm ○ volcanic eruption ○ fog ○ pinpricks ○ crater ○ flames

○ constricting mantle ○ **other form:** _____

. Does the feeling want to do something or act out ? If so, feel free to do

punch a pillow ○ shake yourself ○ scream ○ draw or write something ○
pull a blanket over your head ○ yawn ○ **something else:** _____

. Does it want to tell you something or do words appear inside you?
What has this feeling always wanted to say and get rid of?:

_____
_____

♡ *Take a moment and hold this side of you, understand it, talk to it, take it
seriously* ♡

3. **Do images and/or memories come up?**
○ no → continue with question 9
○ yes → go into them mentally:
Consider the environment of the situation, relive the memory as an observer,
acknowledge the emotions at the time, intuitively change the memory
positively, e.g. with the help of an adult.

9. **Do you feel anything different now than you did in question 2?**
○ disappointment ○ envy ○ anger ○ sadness ○ boredom
○ frustration ○ joy ○ despair ○ helplessness ○ neutral
○ other feeling: _____
*Do you find understanding for your feelings? For example, maybe you were really
just disappointed, and angry as a result? Or just angry about something that caused
you to feel powerless?*

_____
_____

10. Do you now see the situation that happened in question 1 with different eyes? How would you describe it in neutral terms?

_____

_____

_____

11. What would Love say to you now? Answer spontaneously ♡

_____

_____

_____

_____

12. If you are also open to spiritual things:
Ask inwardly for spiritual help and just be open to what comes.
You perceive: ○ loving, gentle, quiet words ○ a subtle, touching energy ○ colors that envelop and strengthen you ○ peaceful mood ○ a mental image of light-filled helpers who are simply there ○ golden light flowing into your heart ○ a basic trust in life ○ protective, invisible embrace
○ something else: _____

13. Is there anything you intuitively would like to do right now from your heart? If so, do it very much :)
○ talk to a good friend ○ go to nature ○ drink a tea ○ take a bath ○ clarify a situation from a new, clear perspective ○ be creative ○ do a hobby ○ light exercise ○ listen to music ○ just relax ○ hug yourself ○ be grateful for this healing experience
○ something else: _____

Space for notes, words or pictures that want to express your feelings:

_____

_____

_____

_____

_____

_____

_____

Contact and other products

(in german language)

Website

www.selbstliebe.me

Here you will find the book "Soul Causes of Sugar Addiction" which describes my story and healing journey from addiction. It will soon be translated into English.

Instagram

s.elbstliebe

Facebook

www.facebook.com/Selbstliebe2017

I am also very happy about a dear review on Amazon

Thank You

All Love for you,
Stefanie

Legal Notice

Stefanie Hartl
Karlstr. 29
86415 Mering
Germany

info@selbstliebe.me

Illustrations created with the following apps:
PicsArt
Quote Maker

Translated with www.DeepL.com/Translator (free version)

Coverdesign: Annemarie Illustrations, www.annemarie-illustrations.com

Image source: Shutterstock

Made in the USA
Las Vegas, NV
22 November 2024

12413945R00079